T0278337

Ukrainian Resistance to Russian Disinformation

Lessons for Future Conflict

TODD C. HELMUS, KHRYSTYNA HOLYNSKA

Prepared for the Office of the Secretary of Defense
Approved for public release; distribution is unlimited

NATIONAL DEFENSE RESEARCH INSTITUTE

For more information on this publication, visit **www.rand.org/t/RRA2771-1**.

About RAND

The RAND Corporation is a research organization that develops solutions to public policy challenges to help make communities throughout the world safer and more secure, healthier and more prosperous. RAND is nonprofit, nonpartisan, and committed to the public interest. To learn more about RAND, visit www.rand.org.

Research Integrity

Our mission to help improve policy and decisionmaking through research and analysis is enabled through our core values of quality and objectivity and our unwavering commitment to the highest level of integrity and ethical behavior. To help ensure our research and analysis are rigorous, objective, and nonpartisan, we subject our research publications to a robust and exacting quality-assurance process; avoid both the appearance and reality of financial and other conflicts of interest through staff training, project screening, and a policy of mandatory disclosure; and pursue transparency in our research engagements through our commitment to the open publication of our research findings and recommendations, disclosure of the source of funding of published research, and policies to ensure intellectual independence. For more information, visit www.rand.org/about/principles.

RAND's publications do not necessarily reflect the opinions of its research clients and sponsors.

Library of Congress Cataloging-in-Publication Data is available for this publication.

ISBN: 978-1-9774-1-3987

Cover image: JANIFEST, used with permission.

About This Report

Since Russia's invasion of Ukraine in February 2022, Russia has waged a wide-reaching, high-volume, and multichannel disinformation campaign that seeks to not only undermine Ukrainian resilience but also gird Russian support for the war and deplete international support of Ukraine. This report provides an overview of Ukrainian efforts to counter this disinformation war and identifies relevant lessons for the United States and allied militaries. The research reported here was completed in April 2024 and underwent security review with the sponsor and the Defense Office of Prepublication and Security Review before public release.

RAND National Security Research Division

This research was sponsored by the Office of the Secretary of Defense and conducted within the International Security and Defense Policy Program of the RAND National Security Research Division (NSRD), which operates the National Defense Research Institute (NDRI), a federally funded research and development center sponsored by the Office of the Secretary of Defense, the Joint Staff, the Unified Combatant Commands, the Navy, the Marine Corps, the defense agencies, and the defense intelligence enterprise.

For more information on the RAND International Security and Defense Policy Program, see www.rand.org/nsrd/isdp or contact the director (contact information is provided on the webpage).

Acknowledgments

The authors would like to express their appreciation to the Ukrainian representatives of government and civil society who offered their profound experience and wisdom in support of this effort. We are also grateful to others who lent their wisdom and experience, as well as to J. D. Maddox of Inventive Insights LLC and Elina Treyger of RAND, who offered insightful comments on a previous draft of this report.

Summary

Russia has disseminated large volumes of false content targeted at Ukrainians, those living in Russia, and global audiences, including those in the United States and Europe. Both Russia's attempts to sow false narratives and the Ukrainian response during the war provide a unique laboratory for considering how nations can counter disinformation and propaganda during conflict. This report seeks to distill some of those lessons. It offers a broad case study of Ukraine's information and counterdisinformation war and highlights key lessons that can help the U.S. national security establishment prepare for and counter disinformation during U.S. contingency operations.

In Chapter 2 of this report, we detail some of the key components of the Ukrainian campaign to counter Russian disinformation and promote pro-Ukraine narratives. It begins by reviewing key initiatives launched before the war, referred to as shaping operations. Key measures taken before the war include a robust effort in Ukraine, prompted by the 2014 Russian invasion of Crimea, to build both government and civil society institutions capable of countering adversary disinformation; unique steps to stop the flow of Russian propaganda targeting the country; and an intelligence-driven "prebunk" that informed Ukrainian and international audiences about a planned Russian operation to falsify a Ukrainian attack on its forces and thereby provide a casus belli for the Russian invasion.

During the war, Russia targeted a variety of audiences with false narratives, to include its own domestic audience, Ukrainians, and the international community. Ukraine has had to counter such narratives across what we call the three theaters of Ukraine's information war. Inside Ukraine, Russia has sought to undermine Ukrainian unity and sap their will to fight. To fight such narratives, Ukraine has responded with a diverse campaign that enlisted both government and civil society institutions to debunk Russian disinformation, prebunk emerging narratives, build the capacity of key frontline communities, and promote media literacy education among the populace. Overall, we find that such efforts seem to have proved largely successful, although countering Russia's narratives targeting frontline communities has been challenging.

Internationally, Russia has worked to undermine the cohesion of international support for Ukraine, targeting seams in domestic U.S. support and working to undermine support in the broader Global South. Ukrainian narratives hailing from the internationally popular President Volodymyr Zelenskyy as well as a band of online Ukrainian influencers helped to enlist early international support while Ukrainian civil society organizations have worked to maintain international support. These efforts proved crucial to galvanizing early support for Ukraine and helped promote international financial, humanitarian, and military support for the country, although cracks in the international coalition have emerged of late.

Finally, the most challenging theater for Ukraine has been inside Russia, where it has attempted to counter strong support for the country's war effort. The Kremlin has limited the Russian population's access to foreign news and social media content and has instituted draconian laws intended to prevent local resistance to the war. While Ukraine has attempted to undercut Russian support by highlighting the costs of the conflict to both Russian soldiers and Ukrainian citizens, such efforts have largely proved unsuccessful.

What lessons can the United States learn from this conflict for its own efforts to counter adversary disinformation during U.S. military contingency operations? First, we note that disinformation is an indispensable tool of warfare, and it seems reasonable to expect that future U.S. adversaries will make use of this tool to target U.S. forces directly, undermine host nation support for U.S. operations, and undercut international coalitions. Beyond this general finding, we offer 12 specific lessons for the United States below, and in greater detail in Chapter 3:

- **Prepare for three theaters of information war:** The United States will need to consider all three of the theaters of information war in planning and preparations for future conflict. The United States should consider innovative ways to reach and communicate with populations residing in totalitarian countries like Russia or China; rally international institutions to more effectively identify, debunk, and prebunk adversary campaigns targeting the rest of the world; and support a broader array of institutions residing in host nations.
- **Build critical host nation institutions in advance of and during conflict:** U.S. and allied governments should look to identify key at-risk

countries early, be they the Baltic nations that sit on Russia's doorstep in Eastern Europe or Taiwan. The goal, as in Ukraine, is a civil society and government that have the necessary skills and resources to counter foreign disinformation and the interconnections to coordinate such efforts.

- **Build and maintain U.S. capacity to counter disinformation:** The United States will need to assess its own doctrine, training, and wargaming efforts to ensure it is able to counter disinformation during conflict. It will also need to ensure that institutions critical to such efforts, like the Global Engagement Center and psychological operations forces, retain their capability.

- **Invest in and work with civil society:** Host nation civil society organizations play a critical role in countering disinformation and can serve as a force multiplier for U.S. forces. The U.S. military, as well as the Department of State, should not only invest in building civil society organizations in advance of future conflict but support and be willing to work closely with such institutions when conflict does arise.

- **Build and maintain trust:** Disinformation most takes root in societies where populations lack requisite trust in government and other key institutions. Because of this, the U.S. government will need to diligently maintain that trust (with host nation as well as international audiences) in order to effectively dispel adversary narratives.

- **Work with and empower local and military influencers:** Social media posts generated by wide swaths of Ukrainian society played a critical role in building international support for Ukraine and establishing a well of support that may have helped buttress against Russia's internationally focused disinformation campaign. The U.S. military and broader U.S. government should strategically seek to promote such online voices to help support U.S. national security objectives.

- **Build resilience of U.S. troops:** Frontline soldiers are a frequent target of adversary campaigns to undermine the will to fight and unit cohesion. The ability of adversaries to target such troops with social media supercharges such efforts. The U.S. military should develop a mandatory media literacy education campaign that can help both deployed and garrison personnel recognize malign influence attempts and foster safer online behavior.

- **Do not allow coordination to sacrifice speed in responding:** Countering adversary disinformation requires efforts that can effectively monitor a large array of potential communication channels and quickly identify and respond to emerging narratives. While efficient use of resources and effective coordination and synchronization of such efforts is ideal, the Ukrainian experience highlights the value of a loosely coordinated and redundant network response that involves multiple actors both monitoring media and communicating key narratives.
- **Be prepared to take risks:** Ukrainian communication efforts have partly been successful because they take risks: They use irreverent humor, with government communicators at times outsourcing their efforts to creative and agile civil society institutions. However, U.S. government communication efforts are notoriously risk averse and involve significant bureaucratic approval processes. Senior U.S. government leaders must be willing to accept risk and allow communicators to quickly (without obtrusive senior leader approval chains) create unique, humorous, and engaging content.
- **Plan on resourcing and executing three critical counterdisinformation tools:** Debunking (fact checking), prebunking, and the promulgation of proactive information narratives will prove critical tools for countering and mitigating the impact of adversary disinformation. Overall, the U.S. Department of State, as well as the U.S. military, will need to ensure that these three approaches are effectively resourced, implemented, and integrated in military theaters of operation.
- **Be prepared to build the capacity of key institutions:** In future contingency operations, the U.S. military and State Department will need to closely consider adversary targets for propaganda and disinformation and evaluate the ability of local institutions, be they government or civil society, to effectively respond. Where needed, the United States can work with host nation experts to conduct trainings and buttress the capacity of the local institutions.
- **Recognize the risk of waning support over time:** As the time engaged in conflict increases, the influence of U.S. messaging may decrease, and adversary disinformation narratives may become more influential. The United States should wargame such risks and consider incorporating them in war plans.

Contents

CHAPTER 1

Introduction

Nation-states have increasingly turned to the sowing of false narratives and online influence operations as a tool of statecraft. The Oxford Internet Institute, for example, identified 81 nations that used government or political party actors to manipulate online opinions. This figure is up from 70 identified in 2019, 48 in 2018, and 28 in 2017.[1] In addition, Diego Martin and colleagues documented a significant rise in the number of influence campaigns "advocating controversial viewpoints and spreading disinformation," from 1 detected in 2011, to 18 and 16 in 2016 and 2017, respectively. Thirty such campaigns were ongoing as of 2020. Russia, Iran, and China—key U.S. adversaries—were among the most prolific in authoring such campaigns.[2]

With this rise in internet-enabled disinformation, we can already observe that warfare will not be immune from such efforts. Russia famously and systematically operationalized disinformation in its cold war against the United States.[3] False narratives were a common refrain in the Syrian war and included false claims about the White Helmets, the Syrian humanitarian organization that worked to save victims of Syrian air strikes, as well as denials about Syrian use of chemical weapons.[4] False narratives about the

---

[1] Samantha Bradshaw and Philip N. Howard, *The Global Disinformation Order: 2019 Global Inventory of Organized Social Media Manipulation*, University of Oxford, 2019.

[2] Diego A. Martin, Jacob N. Shapiro, and Julia G. Ihardt, "Introducing the Online Political Influence Efforts Dataset," *Journal of Peace Research*, Vol. 60, No. 5, November 2022.

[3] Thomas Rid, *Active Measures: The Secret History of Disinformation and Political Warfare*, Farrar, Straus and Giroux, 2020.

[4] Institute for Strategic Dialogue, "ISD's Digital Investigation on Syria Disinformation," webpage, July 13, 2022.

threats to Russian-speaking Ukrainians in the east and south of Ukraine fueled the annexation of Crimea and start of the war in Donbas.[5] The Israeli war against Hamas, spurred by the October 7 Hamas attack against Israeli settlers, has also proved a breeding ground for false claims.[6] Indeed, the 2,500-year-old maxim "In *war, truth is the first* casualty," attributed to Aeschylus, the father of Greek tragedy, remains as true as it ever was.

The U.S. military has not been immune from disinformation targeting its forces. Russia has also worked to undermine the Enhanced Forward Presence battalions of the North Atlantic Treaty Organization (NATO) operating in Estonia, Latvia, Lithuania, and Poland. Russian broadcast television and online news sites would target Russian speakers residing in the region and attempt to sow doubt about NATO and its forces.[7] A forged letter released in 2020 falsely suggested that Polish brigadier general Ryszard Parafianowicz criticized U.S. force participation in the exercise Defender-Europe 20. Russia also attempted to falsely suggest that the U.S. military ignored coronavirus disease 2019 (COVID-19) travel restrictions for the same exercise.[8] Finally, U.S. troops in garrison have also been the frequent target of foreign disinformation, with Russia targeting military personnel as part of its campaign to undermine the 2016 U.S. election. Numerous Facebook groups targeting current and former U.S. military personnel have been shown to be run by administrators based in Europe and Vietnam.[9]

The Government Accountability Office, in a survey of information threats to U.S. forces, highlighted three kinds of malign information: disin-

---

[5] NATO Strategic Communications Centre of Excellence, *Analysis of Russia's Information Campaign Against Ukraine*, 2015.

[6] Todd C. Helmus and William Marcellino, "Lies, Misinformation Play Key Role in Israel-Hamas Fight," *RAND Blog*, October 31, 2023.

[7] Todd C. Helmus, Elizabeth Bodine-Baron, Andrew Radin, Madeline Magnuson, Joshua Mendelsohn, William Marcellino, Andriy Bega, and Zev Winkelman, *Russian Social Media Influence: Understanding Russian Propaganda in Eastern Europe*, RAND, RR-2237-OSD, 2018.

[8] Meghan Fitzpatrick, Ritu Gill, and Jennifer F. Giles, "Information Warfare: Lessons in Inoculation to Disinformation," *U.S. Army War College Quarterly: Parameters*, Vol. 52, No. 1, 2022.

[9] Kristofer Goldsmith, *An Investigation into Foreign Entities Who Are Targeting Servicemembers and Veterans Online*, Vietnam Veterans of America, 2019.

formation, misinformation, and malinformation. *Disinformation* refers to intentionally false or fabricated information, *misinformation* refers to false information that is unintentionally shared, and *malinformation* refers to true information that is presented out of context with the goal of inflicting harm on an individual or organization.[10]

Adversary disinformation (and other forms of malign information) poses a number of potential threats to future U.S. and allied contingency operations. It can be used to undermine international support for such operations and fray international alliances critical to multinational campaigns. It can potentially sap a host nation's popular will to resist foreign invasions or spur resistance and even attacks against U.S. force presence. It can also work to undermine unit cohesion and individual soldier will to fight. For these reasons, it is critical that the U.S. military, together with its interagency partners, develop the capacity to detect and counter adversary disinformation campaigns during conflict.

The blood-drenched war in Ukraine provides a laboratory to better understand not only how adversaries use disinformation during conflict but also how the United States can begin to counter it. First, Russia, relied extensively on disinformation as a tool of war, disseminating large volumes of content targeted at a host of audiences, from those living in Russia to Ukrainians living on the front lines and to U.S. and European citizens watching the war from afar.[11] As the *New York Times* bureau chief in Ukraine observed,

> What is clear is that misdirection, disinformation and propaganda are weapons regularly deployed in Russia's war in Ukraine to buoy spirits at home, demoralize the enemy or lead opponents into a trap. And it is often hard to know when reports are false or why they may have been disseminated.[12]

---

[10] U.S. Government Accountability Office, *Information Environment Opportunities and Threats to DOD's National Security Mission*, GAO-22-104714, September 2022.

[11] Roman Osadchuk, *Undermining Ukraine: How the Kremlin Employs Information Operations to Erode Global Confidence in Ukraine*, Atlantic Council, 2023.

[12] Andrew E. Kramer, "Disinformation Is a Weapon Regularly Deployed in Russia's War in Ukraine," *New York Times*, September 26, 2023.

Ukraine has also been heralded as a success case in countering Russian disinformation. Ukraine has responded to Russian disinformation with persuasive appeals from its leader, President Volodymyr Zelenskyy; disseminated compelling social media content demonstrating Ukrainian resilience; and worked to counter Russian narratives seeking to sap the country's will to fight. Overall, Russia, at least for the first year and a half of the war, failed to thwart a robust international campaign designed to support Ukraine with money, weapons, and humanitarian support.[13] The government of Ukraine has maintained domestic support for the war, and the population remains relatively unified in opposition to the Russian invasion.

The purpose of this report is to examine the lessons that Ukraine offers to the United States and its NATO partners for countering disinformation during conflict. To conduct this study, the authors visited Kyiv, Ukraine, in October 2023 and conducted interviews with representatives of Ukraine's government, military, and civil society. We supplemented these interviews with additional conversations with other experts on the Ukrainian information war as well as select U.S. military personnel experienced in public affairs and information operations.

About This Research

The report first offers a broad case study of Ukraine's information and counterdisinformation war. This case study, presented in Chapter 2, provides an overview of the shaping operations that preceded the 2022 Russian invasion of Ukraine and examines Russian disinformation and the Ukrainian response since the invasion in what we refer to as the three theaters of the information war. These three theaters are Ukraine, the Russian state, and the international arena. This case study is intended not only to serve as a basis for lessons of the war but to also contribute to what is sure to be a future analytic effort to document the history of the conflict and its informational aspects. The report then draws on this case study as well as

---

[13] Missy Ryan, Ellen Nakashima, Michael Birnbaum, and David L. Stern, "Outmatched in Military Might, Ukraine Has Excelled in the Information War," *Washington Post*, March 16, 2022.

4

additional interviews to distill key lessons learned for countering disinformation during military contingency operations. These lessons are presented in Chapter 3. Finally, we offer a conclusion to our report and highlight next steps for research.

It is important to note several limitations inherent to this study. Principally, it is almost certain that no future U.S. military operation will look exactly like the war in Ukraine. Ukraine, which has its own unique history of Russian propaganda and control, is fighting its own war against an invading aggressor. In contrast, the United States is more likely to counter disinformation in the context of different types of lower-intensity missions, including conducting limited military strikes to counter terrorism operations and humanitarian missions. Were the United States to engage in a more heated conflict, it would likely do so as an intervening force, coming to the assistance of NATO partners like Lithuania, Latvia, and Estonia (if Russia were to invade) or defending Taiwan (should China invade). In developing this report's lessons, we attempt to recognize the inherent limits of applying the Ukrainian model, and readers are encouraged to make their own judgments as to the applicability of these lessons to future wars.

CHAPTER 2

The Ukrainian Counterdisinformation Campaign

This chapter seeks to detail some of the key components of the Ukrainian campaign to counter Russian disinformation and promote pro-Ukraine narratives. It begins by reviewing key initiatives launched before the war, referred to as shaping operations, that helped lay the groundwork for successful Ukrainian counterdisinformation initiatives. It then provides a review of the Ukrainian information and counterdisinformation war through the lens of what we call the three theaters of Ukraine's information war. Specifically, we review Ukrainian efforts to counter Russian disinformation inside Ukraine, inside Russia, and in the international community. We find that it seems Ukraine has fared the worst in countering Russia's domestically targeted disinformation inside Russia, and it has by and large experienced success in countering it domestically within Ukraine. Success in the international arena can best be measured in international support for the war, which has slipped over time, maybe particularly so in the United States.

Shaping Operations

Shaping operations seek to, in the words of U.S. Army doctrine, "establish conditions for the decisive operation through the effects on the enemy, other actors, and terrain."[1] Shaping operations in the information domain played a critical role in setting the conditions for Ukraine's successful

---

[1] Army Doctrine Publication 3-0, *Operations*, Headquarters, Department of the Army, 2017, pp. 13–14.

campaigns to both protect domestic audiences against Russian disinformation and enlist international support for its cause. By the time Russia launched its new invasion of Ukraine in February 2022, Ukraine had significantly developed its capacity for countering disinformation. Controversial to some, Ukraine banned a number of Russian broadcast channels and was aided by the release of Western intelligence that undercut a potential Russian false flag operation.

Support and Maturation of Ukraine's Information Space

The story of Ukraine's counterdisinformation fight began in earnest in 2014 with the Revolution of Dignity, or Maidan Revolution, and the Russian invasion of Crimea. In February 2014, Ukraine was engulfed in protests over President Viktor Yanukovych's decision to more closely align with Russia and to not sign a free trade agreement with the European Union (EU). These protests and the violent response from Ukraine's Berkut riot police reached a crescendo in mid-February and ultimately led to the removal of President Yanukovych after he fled the country on February 22, 2014, and the formation of a unity government. Less than one week later, Russia responded with a military invasion of Ukraine's Crimean Peninsula, and it formally annexed Crimea the following month. Soon Russia began militarily supporting Ukrainian separatists in the Donetsk and Luhansk regions of eastern Ukraine (with covert but publicly denied support on the ground from Russian regular military, often referred to as "little green men") in a conflict with the Ukrainian military that would brew up and through its formal 2022 invasion.[2]

Many of the civil society organizations now focused on countering Russian disinformation in Ukraine point to these key events as the impetus for their charter. The Ukraine Crisis Media Center, formed in March 2014, emerged from a nerve center and information clearinghouse for protests against the Yanukovych regime. The center now operates a major international strategic communications hub that seeks to communicate Ukrainian resilience abroad and counter international disinformation about Ukraine.[3]

---

[2] Steven Pifer, "Watch Out for Little Green Men," Brookings, July 7, 2014.

[3] Representatives of the Ukraine Crisis Media Center, interview with the authors, Kyiv, Ukraine, October 24, 2023; Ukraine Crisis Media Center, "Who We Are," webpage, undated.

StopFake was founded at the end of 2013 at the very beginning of the Revolution of Dignity with the goal of uncovering Russian narratives on Ukrainian television channels controlled by Russia-aligned oligarchs. StopFake would quickly gain international renown as a leading fact-checking institution.[4] Detector Media had its start in 2001 analyzing media and assessing journalistic standards but reoriented its focus in 2014 to uncovering Russian disinformation content on TV, radio, and social media and helping Ukrainian audiences resist Russian disinformation. The organization now uses advanced analytics to detect Russian disinformation on Telegram and other social networks.[5] Numerous other organizations, such as VoxUkraine, Texty, and the Institute of Mass Information, similarly pin their start or the opening of a new page in their activities to this time.

The international community played a critical role in supporting Ukraine's information space. International funding was foundational in propping up civil society organizations focused on counterdisinformation. It also helped with coordination. One EU official, for example, noted that the developing civil society sector lacked proper coordination and was competing for resources. International donors including the U.S. Agency for International Development and the European External Action Service helped form the Disinformation Coordination Hub run by the National Democratic Institute (NDI), creating a platform to facilitate more direct interactions among those organizations, which led to the development of formal and informal ties, the exchange of ideas, and opportunities for collaboration.[6]

In 2021, the Ukrainian government formed two institutions that would play a critical role in the 2022 war. One institution was the Center for Strategic Communications and Information Security (CSC) in the Ministry of Culture and Information Policy. At the time, there was a disconnect and lack of coordination between the government and the civil society sector, and the government lacked expertise comparable to what had since matured

---

[4] Representative of StopFake, interview with the authors, Kyiv, Ukraine, October 23, 2023.

[5] Representatives of Detector Media, interview with the authors, Kyiv, Ukraine, October 23, 2023.

[6] Official of European External Action Service, phone interview with the authors, June 21, 2023.

in civil society. The CSC was hence formed to specifically address this gap, and it now operates with a charter to coordinate with and leverage civil society. That same year the government also formed the Center for Countering Disinformation (CCD) within the National Security and Defense Council with the critical mission to identify and counter Russian disinformation narratives. The Armed Forces of Ukraine first began "serious training" in information operations with U.S. and NATO information operators in 2014, and in 2020 they formed the Strategic Communication Department of the Office of the Commander-in-Chief of the Armed Forces of Ukraine (StratCom).[7]

Media literacy education represented another critical shaping tool. With funding from the Canadian government, the educational firm IREX (International Research and Exchanges Board) began a major effort to conduct media literacy trainings in Ukraine. Named Learn to Discern, the program sought to address the demand side of Russian disinformation. Its aim was to help audiences separate fact from fiction, recognize foreign manipulation efforts, and seek out face-based journalism. In a matter of six months, the program's trainings, which began in 2015, reached 15,000 Ukrainians who attended in-person events, 90,000 friends and family of those participants, and some 2.5 million who saw public service announcements and billboard messages.[8] IREX followed this campaign with additional programs that, for example, sought to work in 650 secondary schools by 2021, training teachers and introducing new forms of media literacy curriculum for the classroom.[9]

Banning of Russian Media

In 2017, the Ukrainian government effectively banned access inside Ukraine to the Russian search engine Yandex, the Russian email client Mail.ru, and the social media platform VKontakte (VK), which at the time was Ukraine's

---

[7] Senior specialist at StratCom, interview with the authors, October 23, 2023.

[8] Tara Susman-Peña and Katya Vogt, "Ukrainians' Self-Defense Against Disinformation: What We Learned from Learn to Discern," webpage, IREX, June 12, 2017.

[9] IREX, "Strengthening Media Literacy in the Ukrainian Education System," webpage, undated.

third most visited social media platform in Ukraine after Google and YouTube.[10] Then, in February 2021, President Volodymyr Zelenskyy shut down Ukrainian access to three television channels that were associated with Viktor Medvedchuk, an oligarch with close connections to Russian president Vladimir Putin.[11] Although the bans were controversial, with some experts highlighting the negative consequences of censorship, many Ukrainians interviewed for this report credited the bans with significantly reducing the available volume of Russian disinformation targeting Ukraine.[12] Moral qualms about censorship aside, evidence suggests that although Ukrainians could access VK through the use of virtual private networks, they largely refrained from doing so, and the ban significantly reduced Ukrainian activity on the network.[13] Attesting to the perceived value of such efforts, StopFake's representative observed, "We need to ban Russian info or we lose our country."[14]

Prebunking the False Flag

As Russia's 2022 invasion neared, a key question likely occupied the minds of Russian leaders and planners: How should they justify the imminent attack against Ukraine? A bold-faced invasion would risk galvanizing international support for Ukraine and undercutting the success of the Russian operation. However, if Ukraine were seen to initiate hostilities, then, at least in the minds of some, a Russian response would be warranted. At a minimum, perceptions of a Ukrainian first strike could be enough to weaken

---

[10] Andrew Roth, "In New Sanctions List, Ukraine Targets Russian Social-Media Sites," *Washington Post*, May 16, 2017. See also Yevgeniy Golovchenko, "Fighting Propaganda with Censorship: A Study of the Ukrainian Ban on Russian Social Media," *Journal of Politics*, Vol. 84, No. 2, April 2022.

[11] Peter Dickinson, "Analysis: Ukraine Bans Kremlin-Linked TV Channels," Atlantic Council, February 5, 2021.

[12] Wilson Center, "Media Bans, Free Speech, and Disinformation in Ukraine," webcast event, March 12, 2021.

[13] Golovchenko, 2022.

[14] Representative of StopFake, interview with the authors, Kyiv, Ukraine, October 23, 2023.

pro-Ukraine coalitions or undercut political support for Ukraine in Europe and in the United States.

One means at the Kremlin's disposal to formulate such a justification was to fake a Ukrainian attack in what is referred to as a false flag operation. Russia has a long history of using false flag operations. In 1939, the Soviet Union invaded Finland on the grounds that the Finns had shelled Soviet troops stationed across its border. In reality, the Soviets actually shelled their own troops to enable this casus belli.[15] In 1968, the Soviets used undercover intelligence operatives to fabricate a variety of incidents that helped justify Soviet military intervention in Czechoslovakia and stamp out a rising prodemocracy movement.[16] False flags have further been implicated in Russia's invasion of Georgia in 2008 and its 2014 invasion of Crimea.

Russian plans to stage a false flag operation as a pretext for its invasion of Ukraine, however, were stymied by U.S. intelligence. On January 14, 2022, the U.S. government released information derived from intelligence sources indicating that the Russian government was planning a fake Ukrainian attack.[17] The United States further released intelligence showing that the Russians intended to create a video of an elaborate attack with, according to *New York Times* reporting, "plans for graphic images of the staged, corpse-strewn aftermath of an explosion and footage of destroyed locations"[18] with faked Ukrainian military equipment and Russian-speaking actors in it.[19]

The unique details that were included in the release of U.S. intelligence likely undercut Russian plans for the false flag operation and further warned international audiences to treat subsequent false flag assertions from the Kremlin (including a Kremlin assertion of Ukrainian plans for an assassination of President Putin) with a high degree of skepticism. Such initiatives

---

[15] U.S. Embassy and Consulates in Italy, "How Russia Conducts False Flag Operations," webpage, undated.

[16] Calder Walton, "False-Flag Invasions Are a Russian Specialty," *Foreign Policy*, February 4, 2022.

[17] Natasha Bertrand and Jeremy Herb, "First on CNN: US Intelligence Indicates Russia Preparing Operation to Justify Invasion of Ukraine," CNN, January 14, 2022.

[18] Julian E. Barnes, "U.S. Exposes What It Says Is Russian Effort to Fabricate Pretext for Invasion," *New York Times*, February 3, 2022.

[19] Shannon Bond, "False Information Is Everywhere. 'Pre-Bunking' Tries to Head It Off Early," NPR, October 2022.

are formally called prebunking. They show audiences the types of misleading and false information that they will eventually encounter, with the goal of helping them to recognize and resist it.[20]

Overall, key efforts undertaken during the shaping phase of the war, from the long preparation of Ukraine's counterdisinformation apparatus to the U.S. countering of a potential Russian false flag operation, appeared to undercut Russia's argument for war and positioned Ukraine to more effectively counter Russia's externally focused disinformation during the war.

The Three Theaters of Ukraine's Information War

Since Russia began its full-scale invasion of Ukraine in 2022, three unique theaters for Ukraine's information war have emerged: the bounds of Ukraine proper, Russia, and the rest of the international community. In this section we provide a broad overview of this three-theater information war, highlighting Russian propaganda themes, key counterdisinformation initiatives, and the overall impact of Ukrainian efforts. One caveat we should make concerns our ability to accurately assess outcomes. It is difficult to assess outcomes of such broad information efforts in any scientifically accurate way, especially as there are many factors that combine and interact to affect such outcomes. Consequently, we offer broad assessments based on available data (such as surveys) as well as on the astute observations of interviewees, though we acknowledge their potential bias given that many are intimately involved in Ukrainian information efforts.

Ukraine

We begin by focusing on Russian propaganda efforts inside Ukraine, to include civilian areas under control of Russian occupying forces, the Ukrainian response, and the outcomes of these efforts.

Russian Propaganda

Russia has engaged in a broad-stroke disinformation campaign that uses a variety of tactics to target different sectors of the Ukrainian populace.

---

[20] Bond, 2022.

In line with RAND's prior articulation of Russia's approach as a "firehose of falsehood," Russia has used a variety of tactics to disseminate false narratives, including fake social media accounts, content disseminated via Russian online news channels and the Russian blogosphere, and traditional forgeries.[21]

Many experts interviewed for this report highlighted the critical role of Telegram in enabling Russia's disinformation efforts. Telegram is an alternative social media platform founded by the Russian Pavel Durov. The channel is famously pro–free speech, offering few content moderation policies (aside from restricting child pornography and calls for violence) that could dent its use by disinformation proponents.[22] While only 2 percent of surveyed U.S. adults report using Telegram, it is highly popular in Ukraine, regularly reaching 72 percent of the population in 2023.[23] With Ukraine's restriction of VK as well as pro-Russian television channels, Telegram has become a critical source of Russian propaganda that reaches the Ukrainian population.

Russian propaganda in Ukraine conveys a variety of thematic content that is designed to undermine Ukrainian support for its government and military and the populace's collective "will to fight." Russia also seeks to sow disunity among different sectors of Ukrainian society.[24] In one classic example, a poorly crafted deepfake video was posted on the pro-Russian Telegram that seemed to show President Zelenskyy urging Ukrainians to surrender. Russia has also created fake news videos showing Ukrainians using Nazi symbols or shelling civilian rail stations.[25] Russia has also focused especially on pushing content targeted to local regions. This content often seeks to drive a wedge between Ukrainians by highlighting disparities

---

[21] Christopher Paul and Miriam Matthews, *The Russian "Firehose of Falsehood" Propaganda Model: Why It Might Work and Options to Counter It*, RAND, PE-198-OSD, 2016.

[22] Darren Loucaides, "How Telegram Became a Terrifying Weapon in the Israel-Hamas War," *Wired*, February 8, 2022.

[23] Jacob Liedke and Galen Stocking, "Key Facts About Telegram," Pew Research Center, December 16, 2022; Internews Ukraine, "Ukrainians Increasingly Rely on Telegram Channels for News and Information During Wartime," webpage, November 1, 2023.

[24] Osadchuk, 2023.

[25] Osadchuk, 2023.

in essential services. One such example noted to audiences in Odesa that they lacked the electricity that is abundantly available to citizens of Kyiv.[26]

Propaganda also targets Ukrainian military personnel. Text messages have urged Ukrainian soldiers to surrender and highlighted the unprofessional character of the Ukrainian military, as well as how Ukrainians are unable to use Western-provided weapons.[27] Text messages to frontline troops conveyed the futility of resistance, noting the words of one Ukrainian analyst, "You are just meat, your body will not be found until the snow melts, nobody cares, and you will be killed."[28] Russia also attempted to manufacture rifts between the political and military leadership of Ukraine through a deepfake video of General Valery Zaluzhny, the commander of Ukraine's armed forces, allegedly starting a mutiny.[29] Back in 2014, Russia enabled Wi-Fi access for Ukrainian soldiers to access videos and music online, only to later use the data collected from these soldiers' web traffic to threaten their wives and mothers in real time.[30]

Russia has also worked to influence residents of the territories occupied since the start of the full-scale invasion. Russian actors will make certain websites are accessible to such populations and disseminate leaflets that, for example, highlight specific Telegram channels for these populations to receive targeted news.[31] Russia also deprived Ukrainians access to alternative Ukrainian news sources, such as by restricting websites and jamming Ukrainian radio, which one interview participant described as an "Iron Curtain."[32]

---

[26] Representative of the CSC, phone interview with the authors, June 21, 2023.

[27] Julie Coleman, "Russian Operatives Sent 5,000 Text Messages in a Failed Attempt to Incite Ukrainians to Attack Their Own Capitol," *Business Insider,* April 1, 2022.

[28] Strategic communications expert, interview with the authors, Kyiv, Ukraine, October 24, 2023.

[29] Kateryna Danishevska, "Russians Spreading Deepfakes with Ukraine's Top Officials: How to Distinguish Lies," RBC-Ukraine, November 8, 2023.

[30] Strategic communications expert, interview with the authors, Kyiv, Ukraine, October 24, 2023.

[31] Representative of the CSC, phone interview with the authors, June 21, 2023; strategic communications planner, interview with the authors, Kyiv, Ukraine, October 22, 2023.

[32] Representative of the CSC, phone interview with the authors, June 21, 2023; strategic communications planner, interview with the authors, Kyiv, Ukraine, October 22, 2023.

Ukrainian Activities

Both Ukrainian government institutions and civil society have played a critical role in countering Russian disinformation targeting the country. This effort was supported by the leadership of President Zelenskyy and a host of Ukrainians taking to social media to share messages of support and encouragement.

Government Institutions

As previously noted, there are two primary civilian agencies in Ukraine dedicated to addressing disinformation: the CSC in the Ministry of Culture and Information Policy of Ukraine, and the CCD within the National Security and Defense Council. The CSC has three main lines of operation: developing strategic communications to include narratives that strengthen Ukraine's image, countering disinformation and building resilience toward it, and conducting information campaigns such as those that highlight Russia's aggression.[33] The CSC started to prepare the population even before Russia's full-scale invasion. For example, in June 2021, the CSC created Dovidka.info, an online brochure that seeks to provide "practical tips" for how to survive the war and other threatening situations and protect Ukraine from Russian disinformation.[34] This brochure was also published in print and distributed across Ukraine, with a focus on the eastern territories. After the start of the full-scale invasion, the brochure was updated to address the immediate dangers Ukrainians were facing as well as reiterate the importance of resilience to disinformation.[35]

One of the most notable features of the CSC is its close working relationship with Ukraine's civil society. A representative from the CSC highlighted how the organization draws on the "mutually beneficial" expertise embedded in the civil society organizations, noting, for example, that civil society organizations will reach out to the CSC with ideas about research or counternarratives. The CSC will offer suggestions and help support the

---

[33] Spravdi, "About the Center," webpage, undated.

[34] "An Information Brochure 'In Case of an Emergency or War' Was Presented in Kyiv" ["У Києві презентували інформаційну брошуру 'У разі надзвичайної ситуації або війни'"], *Army Inform*, June 23, 2021.

[35] Dovidka.info, homepage, undated.

initiative with international donors.[36] A representative with the European External Action Service observed that Ukrainian government interfacing and cooperation with civil society organizations proved invaluable to helping the government and civil society "achieve unity of purpose."[37]

The CSC is also working to protect Ukrainians from Russia's hyperlocal disinformation campaign. It accordingly conducts trainings of civil servants in the regional civil military administrations to build their capacity to protect local audiences from Russian disinformation. These civil servants are referred to as "first responders" who are best situated to detect emerging Russian narratives and credibly communicate to local audiences. The three-day trainings focus on frontline areas such as Odesa, Mykolaiv, and Kherson and seek to train administrators to recognize and counter Russian narratives and to prebunk such narratives when possible. They also attempt to network officials from across the frontline communities.[38]

The CSC also helps to communicate with audiences living in the occupied territories, although the effort is fraught. Ukraine, for example, has attempted to use radios in a box, which are portable broadcasting systems of the type that the U.S. military used to communicate with outlying villages in Afghanistan. Although the radio transmitters can reach the occupied areas, Russian jamming and shelling of such radios has undermined their success. Observed a representative of the CSC,

> [Radios in a box] do not work as well in Ukraine as they used to in Afghanistan. You need new solutions, new means of spreading the content. When Russia occupies some part of the land, it builds a solid and hard-to-penetrate information sphere—from the internet to radio to posters. They are crafty.[39]

---

[36] Representatives of the CSC, interview with the authors, Kyiv, Ukraine, October 25, 2023.

[37] Official of European External Action Service, phone interview with the authors, June 21, 2023.

[38] Representatives of the CSC, interview with the authors, Kyiv, Ukraine, October 25, 2023.

[39] Representatives of the CSC, interview with the authors, Kyiv, Ukraine, October 25, 2023.

In contrast, the CCD operates with the primary mandate to monitor Russian disinformation and report findings up through the ministries and their directors and press secretaries.[40] The CCD monitors various media channels, particularly Telegram, and identifies narratives on a weekly basis. Its work started with the RESIST framework, a published model for countering disinformation developed by the British government but ultimately adapted for the CCD's own approach.[41] When the CCD does identify threatening disinformation, it produces an easily read and digestible information memo that gets disseminated to ministry heads or the armed forces. The short memo contains information on the source, a short description of the threat information, information on reach, and recommendations for action (either continued monitoring or a response). In addition, the CCD attempts to assess and identify forthcoming Russian narratives and then considers counternarratives the ministries should use in advance. The agency also works with international parties and, for example, has collaborated with Polish officials on debunking and prebunking Russian disinformation that often attempts to sow division between the nations.

In one example offered by interlocutors within the CCD, the center helped quickly debunk a false story that First Lady Olena Zelenska was spending $1.1 million of Western-provided aid money at a Cartier shop in New York.[42] Upon hearing the rumors, initially spurred by a Nigerian outlet, the CCD reached out to the Office of the President, which shared her itinerary documenting that the First Lady was actually in Canada at the time of the incident. The CCD quickly informed its partners and debunked the false story, preempting any rifts it might have caused.[43]

---

[40] Several months after our interviews, in early 2024, President Zelenskyy appointed a new head of the CCD. Since April 2023, the CCD had had an interim director. It is possible that the new leadership can initiate changes in CCD operations and priorities. Our analysis here focuses on the CCD's mission when we conducted our interviews in October 2023.

[41] James Pamment, "RESIST 2 Counter Disinformation Toolkit," webpage, UK Government Communication Service, 2021.

[42] Tim Norton, "Fact Check: Did Zelensky's Wife Spend $1.1 Million at Cartier in New York?" *Newsweek*, October 5, 2023.

[43] Disinformation expert, interview with the authors, Kyiv, Ukraine, October 2023.

It is notable that both the CSC and the CCD work to identify and respond to Russian disinformation narratives. Even more notable is that several Ukrainians interviewed for this report suggested that the two institutions do not coordinate with each other in any significant way. Indeed, virtually every government ministry has its own strategic communications cell; and Ukrainian ministries, according to multiple interviewees, are notoriously beholden to their own ministers and aligned political factions. One observer described them as "islands" and "castles," and another stated that the two centers "do not collaborate" and "they compete between themselves."[44] The lack of collaboration is most problematic in times of crisis when cooperation is critical. In such a crisis, the representative of one organization observed, "We hit a wall."[45] Still others suggest the system works, if imperfectly. "We have no one hierarchy," observed a strategic communications adviser. "Instead we have a cloud of stratcom bees who fly chaotically. But for some reason they [move in] the [same] general direction. . . . I love this because it reflects the Ukrainian model of [decentralized] strategic communication."[46]

For the military, StratCom coordinates all information activities in this field for the Armed Forces of Ukraine. It works to educate the Ukrainian public, conduct psychological operations against Russian forces, and communicate with international audiences. The military also runs its own television channel, Army TV, on YouTube.[47] To counter Russian propaganda urging Ukrainians to surrender, StratCom worked to highlight the conditions that Ukrainian prisoners of war would face in Russian captivity and how such prisoners returned "tortured [and] exhausted," if they returned at all.[48] They also created explainers to educate Ukrainian troops on Russian disinformation, worked to block sources of Russian messaging,

---

[44] Disinformation expert, interview with the authors, Kyiv, Ukraine, October 2023.

[45] Disinformation expert, interview with the authors, Kyiv, Ukraine, October 2023.

[46] Strategic adviser at International Media Support, phone interview with the authors, June 27, 2023.

[47] Army TV—Ukrainian Military Channel, YouTube, undated.

[48] Anonymous disinformation expert, interview with the authors, Kyiv, Ukraine, October 2023.

and implemented media literacy educational campaigns.[49] The military also provided information to troops about how to deal with stress and gave them recommendations on how to behave in the information sphere, including "what to share, how to behave online, [and] how to talk to their relatives."[50]

The Ukrainian military also attempts, to some degree, to follow the Ukrainian government's One Policy principle and synchronize its communication efforts. According to a report by the Swedish Defence Research Agency, the Ukrainian military coordinates with other Ukrainian government agencies and works to create communication narratives.[51] It also coordinates with civilian agencies like the CSC.[52] When the Territorial Defence Forces develop communications content, they are reportedly required to clear such stories with the Ministry of Defense. However, this same report echoed observations about a "swarm of bees," noting what it described as a "polyphonic, bottom-up type of strategic communication" and highlighting, for example, how, "from brigades to squads, there appear to be a relative vast leeway to convey messages and partake in the overall Ukrainian communications effort in digital media."[53]

Civil Society Organizations

As previously noted, Ukraine had developed a very active civil society sector after 2014 devoted to countering Russian propaganda and disinformation that had rapidly expanded to defend against propaganda efforts directly targeting Ukrainian citizens. These organizations run a variety of programs designed to debunk Russian disinformation narratives and communicate Ukrainian narratives.

VoxUkraine serves as a nonpartisan entity (in that it does not support specific Ukrainian political parties or oligarchs) that seeks in part to moni-

---

[49] Senior specialist at StratCom, interview with the authors, October 23, 2023.

[50] Strategic communications expert, interview with the authors, Kyiv, Ukraine, October 24, 2023.

[51] Ivar Ekman and Per-Erik Nilsson, *Ukraine's Information Front: Strategic Communication During Russia's Full-Scale Invasion of Ukraine*, Swedish Armed Forces, April 23, 2023.

[52] Representatives of the CSC, interview with the authors, Kyiv, Ukraine, October 25, 2023.

[53] Ekman and Nilsson, 2023, p. 43.

tor and counter Russian disinformation. It regularly monitors and debunks false content circulating on Telegram and creates videographic content aired on regional television stations that targets the most damaging and viral Russian content. In one of VoxUkraine's most "efficient" and influential efforts, it also participates in Meta's third-party fact-checking program. It reviews content circulating on Ukrainian Facebook and Instagram and assigns labels to false content.[54] Meta attaches these labels to the relevant Facebook posts and limits the circulation of that content.[55]

Detector Media works to identify Russian propaganda and disinformation, analyze and assess the quality of media content, and build resistance to disinformation. Detector sees itself as an information technology shop and seeks to build artificial intelligence programs that can help detect Russian propaganda. It creates content for satellite television and a ten-minute radio program that is broadcast to occupied territories and provides what is, for some, "the only connection to reality."[56]

Internews Ukraine is an international nonprofit that seeks to promote independent news media and healthy information environments.[57] Internews Ukraine programs are designed in part to tell stories about the resilience of the Ukrainian people, with one program, *The Book of Memory*, conveying firsthand accounts of Russian atrocities and Ukrainian bravery. The program *Kremlin's Voice* highlights Russia's genocidal rhetoric. Internews Ukraine also works as a Meta trusted partner, which enables Internews Ukraine to troubleshoot problems Ukrainians may have with Facebook, such as when Ukrainian accounts are mistakenly blocked by Facebook.[58]

StopFake also works to debunk Russian propaganda and disinformation. It serves, alongside VoxUkraine, as an independent third-party fact checker through the International Fact-Checking Network. Further, in addition to

---

[54] Representative of VoxUkraine, interview with the authors, Kyiv, Ukraine, October 24, 2023.

[55] Meta, "How Meta's Third-Party Fact-Checking Program Works," webpage, June 1, 2021.

[56] Detector Media, homepage, undated.

[57] Internews Ukraine, homepage, undated.

[58] Meta, "Bringing Local Context to Our Global Standards," webpage, January 18, 2023.

publicizing debunked content on its website, it lends its expertise to a variety of other efforts. It contributes material that supports the IREX Learn to Discern program and supports televised fact-checking initiatives.[59] It also offers online tutorials on fact checking, deepfakes, and other online safety initiatives.[60]

Finally, in partnership with local actors, IREX has continued to conduct nationwide media literacy education efforts since Russia's invasion. It has continued its efforts to work in classrooms and build curriculum and teacher capacity reaching 2,127 schools, which is approximately 15 percent of schools in Ukraine. It has also developed a more scalable online media literacy tool that offers variable-length courses. In an effort to motivate Ukrainians to take the short courses during their coffee breaks, IREX branded these courses based on their length, with "espresso" for the shortest course, "Americano" for the middle learning, and "cappuccino with croissant" for the longest short course.[61] The government has also gotten in on the action with the Filter National Media Literacy Project, which aims to help popularize media and information literacy, coordinate media literacy efforts and actors working in the field, and develop the nation's media literacy policy.[62] Filter and IREX also lead a national media test that invites Ukrainians to test their media literacy acumen. In 2023, over 88,000 people took the test, with 13,000 successfully passing it.[63]

Helping tie such varied initiatives together is the Disinformation Coordination Hub supported by the NDI. The Hub serves as a coordination initiative for 48 different local civil society groups, media organizations, and

---

[59] Representative of StopFake, interview with the authors, Kyiv, Ukraine, October 23, 2023; StopFake, "Tools," webpage, undated.

[60] StopFake, undated.

[61] Representative of IREX, interview with the authors, Kyiv, Ukraine, October 22, 2023. According to follow-up communication with this representative of IREX, Kyiv, as of January 31, 2024, over 250,000 Ukrainians had attempted the training exercise, and 17,000 successfully completed it.

[62] Representative of IREX, interview with the authors, Kyiv, Ukraine, October 22, 2023; Filter, "National Media Literacy Project," webpage, undated.

[63] We Dream and Act [Мріємо і діємо], "Summing up the Results of the National Media Literacy Test 2023 . . ." [Підбиваємо Підсумки Національного Тесту з Медіаграмотності 2023 . . ."], Facebook post, November 2, 2023.

government institutions. It includes fact-checking organizations as well as organizations focused on media literacy and broadcasting.[64] The hub meets on an as-needed basis and distributes weekly newsletters highlighting hub member activities. These efforts help organizations to share outreach and research initiatives and cross-pollinate technical knowledge about the detection and communication of disinformation. The hub also serves as a venue for capacity building, with the hub hosting trainings on digital security, artificial intelligence, and more.[65] The RAND team attended one of the hub's gatherings and heard many of the attendees speak in glowing terms about the value of the initiative.[66] The initiative has also led to a number of collaborations between partners. The success of the effort has prompted efforts to develop similar initiatives in Belarus, Moldova, and other Eurasian countries.[67]

Still, with the wide array of civil society organizations operating in Ukraine, together with the various government institutions, there remains a degree of overlap among the programs. Several programs, for example, monitor Telegram and post debunks on their websites. The "swarm of bees" description applies here, as it does to the varying government institutions.

Outcomes

Overall, the Ukrainian internal response to Russian disinformation has been characterized as relatively successful, as evidenced by the interviews with counterdisinformation experts and the polling data. One Ukrainian analyst described Russian disinformation targeting Ukraine as "not effective. . . . Ukrainian audiences don't believe [it]."[68] While this is difficult to measure directly, indicators such as society-level opinions and literacy levels show

---

[64] The Hub meeting that was attended by this study's two authors included such organizations as Internews Ukraine, Wikimedia Ukraine, Resilient Ukraine, LetsData, Ukrainian Security and Cooperation Center, and StopFake.

[65] NDI Disinformation Coordination Hub coordinator, phone interview with the authors, July 11, 2023.

[66] Participants in the NDI Disinformation Coordination Hub, interview with the authors, Kyiv, Ukraine, October 24, 2023.

[67] NDI Disinformation Coordination Hub coordinator, phone interview with the authors, July 11, 2023.

[68] Anonymous Ukrainian strategic communications expert, interview with the authors, Kyiv, Ukraine, date retracted.

the limited impact of Russian efforts in Ukraine. Another analyst noted that "Ukraine's population changed after the full-scale invasion. The awareness and media literacy increased. People can distinguish that the Telegram channel is Russian." Surveys generally bear this out. A report by the National Endowment for Democracy, for example, cited survey data showing that the "percentage of Ukrainians who understood the war in Donbas to be the result of Russian aggression increased from 49 percent in February 2019 to 65 percent in December 2021."[69] In addition, Ukraine maintains strong support for continuing the resistance into 2023, with 60 percent of the surveyed population stating that they want to continue fighting the war until it wins. In addition, a whopping 95 percent of the population remains confident in its military, notwithstanding Russia's efforts to undermine it.[70]

Further, a survey conducted by VoxUkraine in Ukraine suggests promising results of the country's varied counterdisinformation campaigns.[71] A high 97 percent of Ukrainians stated that they are familiar with, understand, or at least have heard of the term *disinformation*. Self-reported confidence in the ability to distinguish disinformation was also related to the level of support for pro-Ukrainian narratives. Ukrainians largely disagreed with pro-Russian disinformation narratives and supported Ukrainian messages. However, pointing to a major challenge for Ukrainians, disagreement with Russian narratives was least pronounced in both the South and the East, where much of Russian disinformation is concentrated.[72] At the same time, while the number of those supporting unification or deeper ties with Russia was higher in these regions, these attitudes fluctuated, barely reaching the majority population after 2014 and often falling after yet another Russian

---

[69] Representative of the National Endowment for Democracy, phone interview with the authors, November 3, 2023.

[70] Benedict Vigers, "Ukrainians Stand Behind War Effort Despite Some Fatigue," Gallup, October 9, 2023.

[71] Alina Tropynina, "The Ability of Ukrainians to Distinguish Messages of Russian Propaganda: Results of Public Opinion Research," VoxUkraine, June 26, 2023.

[72] For example, the statement, "Ukrainians and Russians are fraternal nations or even one nation," was rejected by 88 percent of those surveyed in western Ukraine but rejected by only 70 percent in the East. Ilona Sologoub, "Attitudes of Ukrainians Towards Russia and Russians Towards Ukraine" ["Stavlennia ukraintsiv do Rosii ta rosiian do Ukrainy"], VoxUkraine, June 24, 2023.

statement or action.[73] Research also suggests that measured levels of media literacy increased significantly. The nongovernmental organization (NGO) Detector Media, for example, created a 42-index measure of media literacy and surveyed Ukrainians in both 2020 and 2022. It found, for instance, that the percentage of surveyed adults with what it described as "above-average levels of media literacy" increased from 55 percent to 81 percent.[74]

How successful are the individual government or civil society programs? Overall, it seems there have been limited efforts to document the impact of individual programs on Ukrainian attitudes and behavior. Some initiatives can rely on established scientific consensus. Several studies, for example, have demonstrated the general effectiveness of initiatives that label false posts on social media (of the like implemented with Meta by VoxUkraine and StopFake), with such labels working to mitigate belief in false social media posts.[75] Research also shows the effectiveness of media literacy promotion efforts, and IREX has previously conducted its own research showing the effectiveness of its Learn to Discern intervention.[76] The CSC also conducts pre- and post-surveys with local government leaders whom it trains to counter Russian disinformation.

For a number of initiatives such as fact-checking programs, it is difficult to measure anything other than reach (the number of people who view a webpage or social media post) or engagement (the number who like, share, or comment on social media). As observed by one civil society representative, "The only measurable [indicator of success] is reach, when we had a million, not several thousand. We cannot measure the quality and deepness of engagement. . . . Polls are expensive for a small organization."[77]

Finally, we should note that one analyst interviewed for this report commented that Russian disinformation in Ukraine yielded what she described

---

[73] Sologoub, 2023.

[74] Detector Media, "Media Literacy Index of Ukrainians: 2020–2022," webpage, April 21, 2023.

[75] N. Walter, J. J. Brooks, C. J. Saucier, and S. Suresh, "Evaluating the Impact of Attempts to Correct Health Misinformation on Social Media: A Meta-Analysis," *Health Communication*, Vol. 36, No. 13, November 2021.

[76] IREX, "Learn to Discern," webpage, undated.

[77] Anonymous civil society representative, interview with the authors.

as cumulative effects. That is, over time, as Russia disseminates consistent disinformation themes, some of those themes are slowly gaining traction. As evidence for this, she offered the fact that Russia continues to promulgate narratives that have long been debunked not only by Ukraine but by many respectable institutions, such as that regarding the oppressed status of the Russian language and Russian speakers in Ukraine.[78] We do not have independent evidence for this specific assertion, but the notion of a "cumulative" impact of false narratives does have scientific backing. A body of scientific research consistently demonstrates the illusory truth effect, which refers to the fact that as false narratives are repeated over time, audiences are more prone to believe in them.[79] This can take place even when the false information is initially debunked. The concept might suggest that as the war continues, the Ukrainian populace (and international populations) may be more at risk of adopting views consistent with Russian propaganda narratives.

Russia

A second critical theater for the information war is in Russia, with Ukraine seeking to undermine Russian support for war. Here, Ukrainian efforts, as far as we can tell, have not been notably successful.

Russian Propaganda

Early in the war, Russia blocked access to a number of Western social media platforms, including Facebook and Twitter.[80] The news outlets operating from outside Russia, such as BBC, Deutsche Welle, Voice of America, and Meduza, have also been cut off.[81] The ban also included some Russian domestic media, such as Novye Izvestiya, Ust Kut 24, Permdaily.ru, and

---

[78] Representative of Umbra Research, phone interview with the authors, May 1, 2024.

[79] See, for example, Aumyo Hassan and Sarah J. Barber, "The Effects of Repetition Frequency on the Illusory Truth Effect," *Cognitive Research: Principles and Implications*, Vol. 6, December 2021.

[80] Dan Milmo, "Russia Blocks Access to Twitter and Facebook," *The Guardian*, March 4, 2022.

[81] Anton Troianovski and Valeriya Safronova, "Russia Takes Censorship to New Extremes, Stifling War Coverage," *New York Times*, March 4, 2022.

Kavkazsky Uzel.[82] The Russia-affiliated search giant Yandex demoted content critical of Russia.[83] As it touted its "special military operation," a phrase intended to evoke a limited and specialized operation, Russia also created new laws, empowered with 15-year prison sentences, that forbade criticism about the conflict or even references to it as a "war" or "invasion."[84] Russia also created fake fact-checking sites that helped promote false Russian narratives about the war and hosted specially tailored rallies intended to convey broad support for the war.[85] Ample funding has been provided to propaganda outlets such as Dialog.[86] These already draconian measures have been even further intensified before the presidential election, with the government cracking down on any attempts to access or provide information alternatives to the government messaging.[87]

Ukrainian Information Operations

Ukraine has implemented a number of measures designed to undermine Russian support for the war. Early in the war, Ukraine fielded the Come Back Alive hotline, which was intended to provide families of Russian soldiers an opportunity to check whether their loved ones were either killed or captured by Ukrainian forces.[88] Representatives of the Ukrainian government, including President Zelenskyy, have made direct appeals to Russian citizens to withdraw their support for the war and emphasized the deadly

---

[82] "Russian Media Regulator Blocks More Online News Sources over Coverage of Ukraine War," Radio Free Europe/Radio Liberty, March 16, 2022.

[83] Jacqueline Malaret and Ingrid Dickinson, "Yandex Suppresses Ukraine War Information for Russian Internet Users," Medium, March 31, 2022.

[84] David Gilbert, "Russia Can Now Jail People for 15 Years for Tweeting About the War on Ukraine," Vice, March 4, 2022.

[85] Osadchuk, 2023.

[86] "How the Kremlin's Internet Propaganda HQ Operates," The Bell, September 27, 2023.

[87] "Putin Approves New Media Restrictions Ahead of Presidential Election," Al Jazeera, November 14, 2023.

[88] Amani Nilar, "Ukraine Defence Ministry Sets Up Hotline for Family Members of Russian Soldiers," News 1st, February 27, 2022.

threat that awaits newly mobilized Russian soldiers.[89] In addition, Ukrainian volunteers have worked to trawl through Russian websites and leave comments critiquing the war. In an attempt to reach the largest Russian audience, Ukraine has also launched the FREEDOM TV network with 24/7 Russian-language broadcasting on YouTube; and links to the videos and headlines are shared across a variety of social media, such as Telegram.[90] There have been several criticisms of this initiative, primarily focusing on its cost effectiveness.[91] At the same time, some Ukrainian organizations, including Detector Media and the Institute of Mass Information, acknowledged that its products do reach very high viewership levels from abroad, with Russia being at the top of the list.[92]

Ukraine also targeted Russian troops with leaflets and text messages, urging them to surrender and highlighting the positive treatment that they would receive from the Ukrainian army.[93] Emphasis was placed by Ukraine on exposing the lies of Russian political and military leadership. This was done often in subtle ways, by spreading messaging that on its surface was not directly antiwar but more subtly explored themes that Russians were known to be concerned about, like casualties or corruption.[94] Early in the

---

[89] Alyssa Demus, Khrystyna Holynska, and Krystyna Marcinek, *The Nightingale Versus the Bear: What Persuasion Research Reveals About Ukraine's and Russia's Messaging on the War*, RAND, RR-A2032-1, 2023.

[90] FreeDom, "About Us," webpage, undated.

[91] Daryna Synyts'ka, "Over UAH 900 Million Were Paid for Telethons and Programs for 'Dom,' FreeDom and The Gaze" ["Понад 900 млн грн за рік заплатили за телемарафони й програми для 'Дому,' FreeДом та The Gaze"], *Dozorro*, February 22, 2024.

[92] Nataliya Dan'kova, "How 'FreeDom' Works on the Maidan in Russia and Helps Russians Surrender. Discussion at National Media Talk" ["Як 'FreeДом' працює на Майдан у Росії та допомагає росіянам здаватися в полон. Дискусія на National Media Talk"], Detector Media, October 15, 2023; Oleksandr Ruban, "Domestic Foreign Broadcasting of Ukraine. Whom Do the State TV Channels 'Dim' and 'FreeDom' Broadcast To?" ["Внутрішнє іномовлення України. На кого мовлять державні телеканали 'Дім' і 'FreeДом'"], webpage, Institute of Mass Information, December 4, 2023.

[93] Strategic communications expert, interview with the authors, Kyiv, Ukraine, October 24, 2023.

[94] Julian E. Barnes and Edward Wong, "U.S. and Ukrainian Groups Pierce Putin's Propaganda Bubble," *New York Times*, April 13, 2022.

war, Ukraine's General Staff created a series of videos titled "He's Not in Training," featuring captured Russian soldiers who had been deceived into fighting by Russian leadership.[95] The messages urged Russian soldiers to return home to worried families and emphasized that fighting Ukraine was not their choice.

These efforts to reach Russian military audiences intensified as Russia's large-scale mobilization of additional reserve forces was launched in late September 2022. The focus of Ukraine's information efforts shifted toward the treatment of soldiers as expendable cannon fodder as well as the success of Ukraine's attacks against these forces, which destroyed Russian equipment and led to many casualties. These themes were further amplified by declassified intercepts of phone calls and other communications of Russian troops in Ukraine that were publicly released. While the authenticity and completeness of these intercepts remain unclear, the main message sent by these efforts to Russian current and prospective soldiers was of the horrors and chaos taking place on the battlefield.[96] In October 2022, as most mobilized Russian soldiers were moved to the front line, Ukraine's General Staff published a new video showing Ukraine's might and emphasizing the lack of clear goals for the Russian invasion of Ukraine.[97] At about the same time, Ukraine's military intelligence created a hotline, I Want to Live, for Russian soldiers who are considering defecting. In addition to the phone line, there is also a website and a chatbot in messaging apps.[98] As of early January 2024, the phone hotline had received 26,000 calls, and the website was visited 46 million times from inside Russia.[99] Leaflets with informa-

---

[95] Demus, Holynska, and Marcinek, 2023.

[96] Tom Balmforth and Filipp Lebedev, "Ukrainian Intercepts Show Russian Soldiers' Anger at Losses, Disarray," Reuters, September 5, 2023.

[97] ArmyInform, "What Are You Fighting For?—The Ukrainian Military Has Published an Urgent Appeal to Russian Soldiers" ["За що ви воюєте?—Українські військові опублікували термінове звернення до російських солдатів"], webpage, October 24, 2022.

[98] I Want to Live, "About the Project 'I Want to Live'" ["О Проекте 'Хочу Жить'"], webpage, undated.

[99] Christopher Miller, "'I Want to Live': Russians Defect to Ukraine by Calling Army Hotline," *Financial Times*, January 4, 2024.

tion about this resource have been dropped to Russian positions. All other possible means are being used as well—mass text messages, advertisements on radio and TV, business cards passed out to released prisoners, and even shouts from one trench to another.[100]

Outcomes

Overall, efforts to undermine Russian support for the war do not appear to be successful. For example, surveys of Russian citizens conducted in late 2023 show continued support for President Putin and the war. Most Russians approve of Putin's job performance, and a majority (63 percent) stated that they support Russia's "special military operation" and view the war as a means to "stand against perceived threats from NATO and the West."[101] This is acknowledged by the Levada Center, which also determined that, despite some fluctuations of attitudes toward the peace negotiations, the overall support for the war remains very high.[102]

Many Ukrainians interviewed for this report see the campaign to undermine Russian support as unsuccessful and even futile. StopFake's representative recounted his organization's own efforts to influence the Russian public by translating articles into Russian and enlisting volunteers to leave critical comments on Russian websites and in Russian publications. "We tried to reach audiences [in Russia, but] of course this is not possible. . . . We tried."[103] Another, an officer in the Ukrainian army, observed, "It is hard to change the perceptions inside Russia. No one can do it."[104]

Early in the war, the NGO Join Ukraine enlisted Ukrainians eager to help with the information war. Some joined a movement to support Ukraine's will to fight, and others who spoke English used Twitter accounts to reach

---

[100] Miller, 2024.

[101] NORC, "New Survey Finds Most Russians See Ukrainian War as Defense Against West," press release, January 9, 2024.

[102] "Conflict with Ukraine: Assessments for November 2023," webpage, Levada Center, undated.

[103] Representative of StopFake, interview with the authors, Kyiv, Ukraine, October 23, 2023.

[104] Officer in the Ukrainian Army, interview with the authors, Kyiv, Ukraine, October 23, 2023.

international audiences. But according to one Ukrainian strategic communications expert, "everybody" wanted to join the effort to target Russian citizens to undermine their support for the war. These volunteers would go to Facebook, VK, and Telegram and post about the realities of the war and what was happening to Russian soldiers and try to demoralize them. However, Join Ukraine quickly realized this effort was a "big mistake," as it only united Russians in support of the war. When Ukrainians started "sending them . . . pictures of dead bodies, children, we realized they do not care. The response was that this child had to be killed because it was Nazi."[105] While creativity and entrepreneurship in diversifying and testing messages have helped Ukraine in reaching other audiences, these efforts are unlikely to produce immediate tangible results, hence leading to somewhat pessimistic outlooks. Yet, some evidence suggests that the Russian "iron curtain" might not be as impenetrable as the regime would want it to be. For instance, an analysis of the numbers of Russians downloading virtual private networks and their sentiments expressed on the message boards might indicate that at least the seed of doubt has been planted.[106]

International

The international campaign to counter Russian disinformation is in many ways the most successful and most challenging. Russia has waged a near-worldwide campaign to promote its cause and sow narratives intended to weaken the international coalition. Ukraine scored an early and resounding victory in the information space by galvanizing both U.S. and European support for its cause, but building on these early successes has proved to be challenging as the war has continued.

Russian Propaganda

Since the run-up to the war before its invasion, Russia has marshaled its significant propaganda resources to execute a near-worldwide campaign meant to undermine international support for Ukraine. At the start of the war, Russia's main narrative was focused on branding the Ukrainian

---

[105] Strategic communications expert, interview with the authors, Kyiv, Ukraine, October 24, 2023.

[106] Barnes and Wong, 2022.

people as Nazis. One report found, for example, that Russian-linked social media accounts mentioned the word *Nazi* in more than 5,800 tweets.[107] The campaign, however, failed to resonate and build support for the Russian operation that many saw as a bold-faced violation of international law and Ukraine's sovereignty. The campaign also ran headlong into a growing narrative about Ukrainian resilience and Russian war crimes.

Faced with the potential failure of this campaign, Russia increasingly focused its efforts on fomenting cracks in U.S. and European cohesion and support for Ukraine. In Poland, for example, Russia used a "multichannel, full-spectrum disinformation campaign" that included falsified documents that sought to convey that Poland intended to occupy territories in eastern Ukraine, alongside false claims about rampant criminal acts committed by Ukrainian refugees residing in Poland.[108] Russia also released stories about Ukraine reselling weapons on the black market, French Caesar howitzers being captured by Russian forces, and the threat of cold winters being exacerbated by European cuts in Russian gas imports.[109] Tweets by Russian accounts replaced narratives about Nazi Ukrainians with content emphasizing European energy and increases in the "cost of living."[110] These efforts targeted already-existing polarization in Western European countries, such as Germany, France, and Italy, with the intention of shifting public opinion away from supporting Ukraine. The latter is portrayed as not only harmful to these countries' economies and well-being but also a threat to their national security, dragging them into war and increasing the risk of nuclear escalation.[111] These narratives were disseminated through a net-

---

[107] German Marshall Fund Alliance for Securing Democracy, "ASD Social Data Search," webpage, undated.

[108] Vera Bergengruen, "Inside the Kremlin's Year of Ukraine Propaganda," *Time*, February 22, 2023.

[109] Kate Abnett, "EU on Track to Quit Russian Fossil Fuels—Report," Reuters, October 24, 2023.

[110] Peter Stone, "Russia Disinformation Looks to US Far Right to Weaken Ukraine Support," *The Guardian*, March 16, 2023.

[111] Oleksii Nabozhniak, Oleksandra Tsekhanovska, Andrea Castagna, Dmytro Khutkyy, and Anna Melenchuk, *Revealing Russian Influence in Europe: Insights from Germany, France, Italy and Ukraine*, German Marshall Fund of the United States, 2023.

work of social media channels and accounts as well as by Russia-sponsored "experts" publishing articles or participating in broadcasts on media outlets such as Voice of Europe.[112]

Russian propaganda targeting the United States leveraged a tried-and-true approach of emphasizing themes that could heighten political tensions about support for Ukraine. The U.S. intelligence community, for example, released findings suggesting that Russia sought to "denigrate the Democratic Party" in order to "weaken U.S. support for Ukraine."[113] It pushed conspiracy theories about U.S. bioweapon laboratories in Ukraine and highlighted Putin's support for traditional values and his "fight against 'woke' ideas." It also responded to the removal of Russian content on mainstream social media platforms like Facebook by promoting content on fringe right-wing social media platforms such as Parler, Rumble, and Gab. A number of Russian themes also received attention on Far Right media outlets in the United States.[114] Russia also attempted to leverage reports of Ukrainian corruption to sow mistrust about Ukraine's use of Western funding and support.[115]

A *Washington Post* analysis of leaked Russian documents further highlights the scope and target of Russia's campaign. The campaign has leveraged thousands of social media posts and fabricated articles and websites in order to argue that President Zelenskyy is corrupt, as well as emphasizing the need for the United States to fund border security rather than Ukraine. The documents suggest that Russia began to focus on undermining U.S. support for Ukraine in January 2023 when it called on public relations firms and political strategists to expand their efforts against the United States, with

---

[112] Ido Vock, "Russian Network That 'Paid European Politicians' Busted, Authorities Claim," BBC News, March 28, 2024.

[113] (U) National Intelligence Council, *Foreign Threats to the 2022, U.S. Elections*, December 23, 2022, Declassified on December 11, 2023, p. 7. See also Steven Lee Myers, "Russia Reactivates Its Trolls and Bots Ahead of Tuesday's Midterms," *New York Times*, November 10, 2022.

[114] Stone, 2023; Jessica Brandt, Valerie Wirtschafter, and Adya Danaditya, "Popular Podcasters Spread Russian Disinformation About Ukraine Biolabs," Brookings, March 23, 2022.

[115] Detector Media, "Tactics and Tools: How Russian Propaganda Uses Corruption in Ukraine to Achieve Its Goals," webpage, August 11, 2023.

a specific task being to highlight that "Americans are not ready to sacrifice their well-being for the sake of the conflict in Ukraine."[116]

Russia has also launched a broad campaign to influence the Global South, including India, Africa, and Central and South America. To do so, Russia has leveraged an extensive network of TV programming and social media channels and influencers that operated before the full-scale invasion.[117] These resources were used both to disseminate the same set of narratives about Ukraine and its invasion as in the West (Nazi Ukrainians, Russia was provoked, etc.) and to spread more tailored narratives targeting existing grievances.[118] The effect of the war on Africa and other developing regions was one of the prevailing themes. Blaming the war and the consequences felt by these regions (e.g., food insecurity, rising energy prices, inflation)[119] on Ukraine and the West, Russia attempted to present itself as an anticolonial, anti-imperialist power that is understanding and protecting the interests of African nations. This message was pushed not only through the media but also through numerous visits of the Russian foreign minister to Africa in 2022 and 2023,[120] as well as in Putin's meeting with African leaders in Moscow to discuss a "peace deal" developed by these leaders on the agenda.[121] Other examples of such targeted narratives include the amplification of stories about perceived

---

[116] Catherine Belton and Joseph Menn, "Russian Trolls Target U.S. Support for Ukraine, Kremlin Documents Show," *Washington Post*, April 8, 2024.

[117] Elian Peltier, Adam Satariano, and Lynsey Chutel, "How Putin Became a Hero on African TV," *New York Times*, April 13, 2023.

[118] Grigor Atanesian, "Russia in Africa: How Disinformation Operations Target the Continent," BBC, February 1, 2023.

[119] Bitsat Yohannes-Kassahun, "One Year Later: The Impact of the Russian Conflict with Ukraine on Africa," *Africa Renewal*, February 13, 2023.

[120] Sam Metz and Bouazza Ben Bouazza, "Russia's Foreign Minister Tours North Africa as Anger Toward the West Swells Across the Region," AP News, December 21, 2023; Elian Peltier, "Russia's Foreign Minister Heads to Mali, His Third Trip to Africa in Recent Months," *New York Times*, February 6, 2023.

[121] Mark Trevelyan and Kevin Liffey, "African Leaders Tell Putin: 'We Have a Right to Call for Peace,'" Reuters, July 28, 2023.

racism in Ukraine,[122] and even the recycling of prior Russian disinformation narratives focused on biological weapons, this time claiming that biological testing was conducted on Africans.[123]

Ukrainian Activities

The Ukrainian response to these disinformation efforts in the international arena has involved a wide array of actors, beginning with President Zelenskyy.

Ukrainian Government

President Zelenskyy has proved, by coincidence or democratic design, a highly effective communicator who has been able to unify the Ukrainian populace against the Russian invasion. When Russia disseminated content highlighting how the president fled Ukraine to the west, Zelenskyy responded with his now famous "We Are Here" video, in which he and his team dramatically claimed from Kyiv's city square that they had not fled and were to remain in Ukraine for the duration of the fight.[124] He has also personified a contrast with Russian president Putin, actively visiting frontline combat troops while Putin famously attended staged events and sat alone across an exceedingly long conference table, allegedly out of fear of contracting COVID-19 from his own generals. As one of Zelenskyy's strategic communications advisers noted, the president is a "machine by himself" and offers "very powerful personal skills and has found a way to speak directly" to domestic and international audiences alike.[125]

The Ukrainian government has also implemented a campaign to promote its cause on social media. One success story is the Ukrainian Ministry of Defense (MoD) Twitter account. While democratic Ukrainian governments

---

[122] Mary Blankenship and Aloysius Uche Ordu, "Russian Disinformation in Africa: What's Sticking and What's Not," Brookings, October 17, 2022.

[123] Michael R. Gordon, Gabriele Steinhauser, Dustin Volz, and Ann M. Simmons, "Russian Intelligence Is Pushing False Claims of U.S. Biological Testing in Africa, U.S. Says," *Wall Street Journal*, February 8, 2024.

[124] Valerie Hopkins, "In Video, a Defiant Zelensky Says, 'We Are Here,'" *New York Times*, February 27, 2022.

[125] Strategic communications adviser, interview with the authors, Kyiv, Ukraine, October 24, 2023.

have long recognized the importance of creativity and agility in government communications,[126] the success of the MoD's Twitter account is particularly striking. Early in the war, the ministry handed control of its Twitter account to a Ukrainian NGO staffed by former commercial, government, and civil society strategic communication experts. The account has since accrued over 2 million followers and produced a series of newsworthy posts that troll and mock Russia's armed forces, draw on jaded forms of humor, and speak in culturally relevant ways to critical audiences abroad.[127] One post, for example, showed the length of Ukraine's front line superimposed on a map of Japan that included the Kuril Islands, which are disputed between Tokyo and Moscow. The post resonated heavily in Japan, with comments from Japanese audiences surging in response.[128] In another, the MoD's Twitter account published a thank-you video to the people of France for donating Caesar 155mm howitzers. The video romanticized the French contribution with roses, chocolate, and sexualized images of the "155mm" French contribution and ended with the plea, "Please send us more."[129]

Influencers

Ukrainian social media influencers have played a prominent role in helping to inform international audiences about the war in Ukraine and induce sympathy with the Ukrainian cause. Numerous social media posts, often disseminated by seemingly regular Ukrainians, have gained worldwide attention and helped to tell the story of a resilient underdog defeating a bully foe. Salient examples include a Facebook post featuring a little girl

---

[126] The first success story dates back to the mid-2000s, when President Viktor Yushchenko, elected after the Orange Revolution, "outsourced" the campaigns to raise awareness about the Holodomor in Ukraine. Former president Petro Poroshenko was also working with a group of marketers and strategic communication specialists to promote Ukraine's narratives abroad after the events in 2014, when the information war with Russia moved into a more heated phase, accompanied by the first ground invasion of Ukraine's east and south. Strategic communication advisers, interview with the authors, Kyiv, Ukraine, October 25, 2023.

[127] Mehul Srivastava, "'Trolling Helps Show the King Has No Clothes': How Ukraine's Army Conquered Twitter," *Financial Times*, October 14, 2022.

[128] Srivastava, 2022.

[129] Defense of Ukraine [@DefenceU], "Sophie Marceau . . . Isabelle Adjani . . . Brigitte Bardot . . . Emmanuel Macron! . . . and CAESARs! ▬ ♥ ▍ ▍," Twitter post, October 12, 2022.

named Amelia singing *Frozen*'s "Let It Go" from a bomb shelter,[130] as well as images of Ukrainians stopping tanks with their bodies and farmers using tractors to tow Russian tanks.[131] In similarly striking posts, a parliamentarian posted a photo of herself barefoot in her apartment carrying a rifle,[132] and a young girl posed for a photo wearing a bright-red prom dress amid the rubble of her destroyed high school in Kharkiv.[133] The Ukrainian military has also pursued a similar approach with its own social media, with individual soldiers posting directly. Early in the war, one such post involved a soldier staring straight at the camera, screwing a silencer to the barrel of his Kalashnikov, and telling the camera, "Guys, you're f—ked."[134] Another soldier months later posted a riveting story about his role in the destruction of scores of Russian tanks as they attempted to cross the Siverskyi Donets River.[135] Other soldiers, marines, and airmen have used their social media feeds to share slice-of-life videos from the front lines.[136]

---

[130] Marina Pitofsky, "A Girl Sang 'Let It Go' from 'Frozen' in a Bomb Shelter. Idina Menzel Says 'We See You,'" *USA Today*, March 9, 2022.

[131] Sergei Perfiliev [@perfiliev], "A Ukrainian farmer using his tractor stole A TANK . . . 😂😂😂," Twitter post, February 27, 2022.

[132] Strategic communications expert, interview with the authors, Kyiv, Ukraine, October 24, 2023; Kira Rudik [@kira.rudik], "Ukrainian woman. I love colorful tulips, Pilates, the color pink. Planting flowers, walking until night on Andriivskyi, my cat Michelle. Smelling new perfumes, laughing out loud, wearing soft socks that are a little slippery on the floor. Wiping glasses with a napkin, marshmallows, arranging documents alphabetically" ["українська жінка. Я люблю різнокольорові тюльпани, пілатес, рожевий колір. Саджати квіти, гуляти до ночі по андріівському, свою кішку Мішель. Нюхати нові парфуми, голосно сміятись, носити м'які шкарпетки, які трохи слизькі на підлозі. Витирати серветкою бокали, зефір, розкладати документи за алфавітом"], Instagram post, February 25, 2022.

[133] Anna Episheva [@avalaina], "My niece was supposed to graduate this year from her high school . . . ," Twitter post, June 7, 2022.

[134] Julia Ioffe [@juliaioffe], "'I'll record this in Russian so it's f—ing clearer,' says this happy (Ukrainian) warrior. 'Guys, you're f—ed,'" Twitter post, February 25, 2022.

[135] Defense of Ukraine [@DefenceU], "Artillerymen of the 17th tank brigade of the #UAarmy have opened the holiday season for ruscists. Some bathed in the Siverskyi Donets River, and some were burned by the May sun," Twitter post, May 11, 2022.

[136] Todd C. Helmus, "The Ukrainian Army Is Leveraging Online Influencers. Can the U.S. Military?" *War on the Rocks*, March 1, 2023.

These social media posts and the accounts that share them have served as a force multiplier for Ukraine. They expanded the volume of content that any official account could create and cumulatively reached a far greater audience. The people and personalities behind the accounts also establish a human connection with their followers.[137] This has helped to personalize the content and the war in ways that official, government-produced slick propaganda videos could never match.[138] The result is that many Americans and Europeans are reminded of the war, its costs, and Ukraine's tactical victories every time they scroll through Twitter or TikTok.

Influencers in the military operate relatively independently from official channels, with the MoD imposing only general rules. One Ukrainian officer supporting the MoD's strategic communications referred to this approach as "trust based." "The goal," he says, "is to leverage soldier creativity." Marketing experts and strategic communications advisers in a joint interview observed, "Creativity is also a key to success. You don't have billions of dollars, so you need to be more creative. You do not have money."[139]

This avalanche of viral social media content was aided by a rapid growth in mobile technology, with 89 percent of Ukrainians able to access cell phone internet by 2022, from 4 percent in 2014.[140] But beyond these technological shifts, Ukraine's success in the international narrative space has also been driven by a bottom-up movement enabled by the rapid growth of civil society voices operating with relative independence from the Ukrainian government. Liubov Tsybulska offered one such example of this trend in one of the most viral tweets of the war, a short missive on Twitter about a Ukrainian woman downing a Russian drone with a jar of pickles.[141] Commenting on that viral tweet, a strategic communications expert observed

---

[137] Mia Sato, "Ukrainian Influencers Bring the Frontlines to TikTok," *The Verge*, March 16, 2022.

[138] Helmus, 2023.

[139] Strategic communications advisers, interview with the authors, Kyiv, Ukraine, October 25, 2023.

[140] Joanna York, "'World's First TikTok War': Ukraine's Social Media Campaign 'a Question of Survival,'" France 24, February 2, 2023.

[141] Liubov Tsybulska [@TsybulskaLiubov], "In Kyiv a woman knocked down a Russian drone from a balcony with a jar of cucumbers. How did they expect to occupy this country?" post to the X platform, March 5, 2022.

that "Ukraine survived because of a strong civil society movement. Otherwise, Ukraine would not survive."[142]

Civil Society Organizations

A number of Ukrainian civil society organizations have implemented programs to counter Russian disinformation narratives in the West and promote continued support for Ukraine. One such organization is the NGO Resilient Ukraine, which hosts the We Are Ukraine initiative, an effort that seeks to educate foreign audiences about the Ukrainian nation, its resilience, and the "truth about the war in Ukraine."[143] It shares stories about Ukrainian resilience and culture on its website, on social media, and via a daily newsletter. Its content, according to the NGO's own in-house analytics, reaches over 100 different countries and 50–60 million users on Instagram. It also manages the Business for Ukraine initiative, which campaigns to have Western businesses leave Russia. It is also developing programs to reach audiences in Africa by working through individuals born in Africa "who became successful in Ukraine."[144]

Other programs also work to create and disseminate media content in the West. Internews Ukraine's Ukraine World initiative tells individual stories of Ukrainian resilience that are spread on Instagram and YouTube.[145] The Ukraine Crisis Media Center disseminates a weekly newsletter to international journalists highlighting stories about Ukraine and hosts a YouTube-published talk show, "Ukraine in Flames." It also attempts to communicate with the Global South by creating written products for the region, though analysts admit that it must compete with Russia's own high-volume campaigns targeting audiences in the Global South.

There are also grassroots initiatives. The organization Ukrainian Prism works with the Ukrainian diaspora in Canada and the United States. The goal is to help those in the diaspora effectively communicate about Ukraine

---

[142] Strategic communications expert, interview with the authors, Kyiv, Ukraine, October 24, 2023.

[143] We Are Ukraine, homepage, undated.

[144] Representative of NGO Resilient Ukraine, interview with the authors, Kyiv, Ukraine, October 23, 2023.

[145] Representatives of Internews Ukraine, interview with the authors, Kyiv, Ukraine, October 23, 2023.

and its needs. It also seeks to promote the Ukrainian cause in the Global South, including Latin America, arguing that such efforts are critical if Ukraine is to gain necessary support in international organizations like the United Nations.[146]

Outcomes

The success of Ukraine's international outreach can be measured in part by the attention it has received in both news and social media. In the first days after the initial invasion of Ukraine, attention on social media skyrocketed with over 18 million interactions on social media in response to news articles published about Ukraine, as reported by the news organization Axios.[147] However, after 100 days of war, these interactions declined precipitously to 348,000 daily interactions. News media mentions of Ukraine have met a similar fate, initially reaching a high of 520,000 mentions in the war's first week but declining to 70,000 a week after the war's first 100 days.[148] Google news searches returned to prewar levels after only six months.[149]

A series of surveys conducted by the Pew Research Center highlights both the initial, resounding support offered to Ukraine by the international community after the invasion and the challenge of maintaining that support. International surveys in both January and March 2022 show precipitous declines in support for Russia and its president. Support for Zelenskyy skyrocketed in the United States, with 72 percent of surveyed adults reporting at least "some confidence" in President Zelenskyy and at least 50 percent of both Democrats and Republicans viewing the Russia-Ukraine war as a major threat to the United States.[150]

---

[146] Representatives of Ukrainian Prism, interview with the authors, Kyiv, Ukraine, October 25, 2023.

[147] Neal Rothschild, "World Looks Elsewhere as Ukraine War Hits 100 Days," Axios, June 2, 2022.

[148] Rothschild, 2022.

[149] Martin Armstrong, "Has Ukraine News Fatigue Set In?" webpage, Statista, August 24, 2022.

[150] John Gramlich, "What Public Opinion Surveys Found in the First Year of the War in Ukraine," Pew Research Center, February 23, 2023.

These levels of support propelled the West to donate large sums of financial, humanitarian, and military support to Ukraine. From January 24, 2022, until January 15, 2023, global government-to-government commitments to Ukraine totaled €143 billion (which equals approximately $153 billion). The United States accounted for half of this amount, with a commitment of €73.18 billion (approximately $79 billion).[151]

However, cracks emerged in this support a year later, with only 29 percent of Republicans and 43 percent of Democrats in the United States identifying the war as a major threat. In addition, by January 2023, four out of every ten Republicans reported that the United States provided "too much aid to Ukraine," up from only 9 percent early in the war.[152] By December 2023, nearly half of Republicans reported that the United States was providing too much support to Ukraine.[153] These trends contrast significantly with Europe (as discussed below).

The Kiel Institute for the World Economy has recently noted that between August and October 2023, there was a precipitous decline in newly committed aid to Ukraine, what it described as "an almost 90 percent drop compared to the same period in 2022."[154] There are several obvious factors driving this decline in international support for continued aid to Ukraine. First, opposition has grown in recent months primarily from the ranks of senior Republican leadership in the United States, channeling a worldview that generally eschews funding foreign alliances and partners such as NATO, as well as legacy U.S. involvement in what it calls "forever wars."

---

[151] Christoph Trebesch, Arianna Antezza, Katelyn Bushnell, André Frank, Pascal Frank, Lukas Franz, Ivan Kharitonov, Bharath Kumar, Ekaterina Rebinskaya, and Stefan Schramm, "The Ukraine Support Tracker: Which Countries Help Ukraine and How?" Kiel Institute for the World Economy, Kiel Working Paper No. 2218, February 23, 2023.

[152] Gramlich, 2023.

[153] Andy Cerda, "About Half of Republicans Now Say the U.S. Is Providing Too Much Aid to Ukraine," Pew Research Center, December 8, 2023.

[154] Pietro Bomprezzi, Yelmurat Dyussimbinov, André Frank, Ivan Kharitonov, and Christoph Trebesch, "Ukraine Support Tracker," webpage, Kiel Institute for the World Economy, undated.

Along these lines, former President Donald Trump has not made secret his disdain for funding Ukraine's war against Russia.[155]

In addition, the stalemate on the eastern battle lines in Ukraine has not helped. Before the summer of 2023, expectations were high that a Ukrainian counteroffensive could yield significant gains on the battlefield, but the offensive did not yield the anticipated dividends. The initial and resounding success of Ukraine's defense against the Russian invasion and the excitement generated by Ukraine's success in recapturing Kharkiv and vast swaths of formerly occupied territory in the summer of 2022 has seemingly now grown old. Further, the Hamas terrorist assault against Israeli settlements on October 7, 2023, followed by the resulting Israeli war in Gaza and the humanitarian devastation it has wrought, has now captured the world's attention. All of these factors have understandably sapped U.S. attention and created competition for U.S. military and financial resources in support of Ukraine.

If nothing else, Russian propaganda has sought to leverage these various factors to its advantage by attempting to accentuate democratic divisions inside the United States. Further, consistent Russian promulgation of themes related to, for example, Ukrainian corruption may have generated a cumulative impact on U.S. audiences over time. Scholars have yet to fully explore the impact of Russia's efforts on specific declines in U.S. support for the war, and so its true impact, if any, remains unknown. But these factors do highlight the critical challenge faced by Ukraine in marshaling long-term support for its cause.

Overall, Europe remains more steadfast in its support of Ukraine. The polls show that support for Ukraine more generally, as well as specific measures such as financial aid, sanctions on Russia, or welcoming Ukrainian refugees, remains stable. According to Eurobarometer, in late 2023, 72 percent of respondents in the EU agreed that financial support for Ukraine is necessary, and nine out of ten agreed with the continued provision of humanitarian support to Ukraine.[156] In most European countries, the majority of surveyed citizens (60 percent) also believe that continued mil-

---

[155] Kate Sullivan and Shania Shelton, "Trump Signals Opposition to New Senate Foreign Aid Package," CNN, February 10, 2024.

[156] European Commission, "Europeans Continue to Strongly Support Ukraine, Eurobarometer Shows," webpage, December 13, 2023.

itary assistance can help Ukraine defeat Russia.[157] The two countries that have different views stand out. According to the polling data, respondents in Slovakia were predominantly blaming Ukraine or the West for the war and all its consequences, such as inflation and energy prices.[158] This sentiment is believed to have helped drive electoral victories for pro-Russian politicians in the country in October 2023 (parliamentary elections) and April 2024 (presidential election).[159] The newly elected government halted programs of military assistance to Ukraine, reversing the policy of the previous government, which was a staunch supporter and provided fighter jets and other critically important equipment.[160] Similarly, Bulgaria provided military aid to Ukraine and attempted to limit Russian influence in the country throughout the first year and a half of the war. However, the collapse of the pro-Western government in June 2022 and start of the campaigning for the June 2024 European Parliament elections brought these issues to the forefront, creating an opportunity for pro-Russian politicians and groups to exploit internal rifts and promote anti-Ukraine and anti-West sentiment.[161]

At the same time, the number of those who support ending the war through a negotiated settlement, rather than on the battlefield, has started to increase in other European countries.[162] These changes in public opinion are especially relevant given upcoming elections to the European Parliament. Continued support for Ukraine is among the top issues debated by the opposing political camps across the EU, with centrist parties (center-right and center-left) largely clashing with the populist ones (Far

---

[157] European Commission, 2023.

[158] Emma Bubola, "Slovakia's Election Could Echo in Ukraine. Here's What to Expect," *New York Times*, September 30, 2023.

[159] Radovan Stoklasa and Jan Lopatka, "Pellegrini Wins Slovak Presidential Election in Boost for Pro-Russian PM Fico," Reuters, April 6, 2024.

[160] "New Slovak Government Rejects Final Military Aid Package for Ukraine," Reuters, November 8, 2023.

[161] Antoaneta Roussi and Jacopo Barigazzi, "Expect Russia to Do 'Whatever Possible' to Reassert Influence in Bulgaria, Outgoing PM Warns," *Politico,* April 9, 2024.

[162] Yasmeen Serhan, "As Russian's War Enters Third Year, Optimism for Ukraine Sinks," *Time*, February 23, 2024.

Right).[163] Some countries, such as France, have signed bilateral security agreements with Ukraine already and are pushing for the need to make further support a central topic of the upcoming EU election.[164] From the start of the invasion until early 2024, EU countries made over $101 billion available in assistance and committed to an additional $54 billion to support reconstruction and reforms.[165] This recent commitment was passed, overcoming Hungary's blockade, but the sustainability of these efforts after the elections remains unclear.[166]

In Latin America, the Middle East, and Africa, Russia has sought to leverage anticolonial and anti-Western sentiment to further undermine international support for Ukraine.[167] Using a network of its own ambassadors and directly or indirectly affiliated media outlets, Russia has been pushing narratives about the West exploiting the Global South for economic benefits.[168] The war in Ukraine is presented as an example of Western nations ignoring the needs of the developing world, such that Western nations are blamed for economic hardships faced by the poorer countries. These efforts seem to have paid off in some form, as evidenced by public opinion polling (many countries in the Global South continue to think positively about Russia and agree with its views on the war) and votes in the United Nations General Assembly.[169]

---

[163] Stanley Pignal, "Europe's Elections Pitch Centrists Against Populists, Again," *The Economist*, November 13, 2023.

[164] Ania Nussbaum and Samy Adghirni, "Macron Makes Ukraine Central in the European Election Campaign," Bloomberg, March 12, 2024.

[165] Delegation of the European Union to the United States of America, "EU Assistance to Ukraine (in U.S. Dollars)," webpage, February 22, 2024.

[166] Niklas Ebert, "What's at Stake in the EU Elections: Ukraine Aid," German Marshall Fund of the United States, February 20, 2024.

[167] Digital Forensic Research Lab, "In Latin America, Russia's Ambassadors and State Media Tailor Anti-Ukraine Content to the Local Context," Atlantic Council, February 29, 2024.

[168] Sergey Sukhankin, "Russia Struggles for 'Hearts and Minds' in Global South (Part Two)," Jamestown Foundation, February 23, 2024.

[169] Jochen Kleinschmidt, Artem Miniailo, Rashid Gabdulhakov, and Chelsea Ngoc Minh Nguyen, "Perceptions of Russia's War in the Global South," *Russian Analytical Digest*, Vol. 305, November 30, 2023.

CHAPTER 3

Lessons from the War for Countering Disinformation During Military Contingency Operations

Drawing on this review of Ukraine's effort to counter Russian disinformation, we extract 11 lessons for the U.S. government as it considers how to prepare for and counter adversary disinformation during conflict. These lessons add to those already identified in a growing body of scholarship about the counterdisinformation lessons from Ukraine.[1] We recognize that not all of these lessons will apply to each and every form of future conflict, given that there are different types of operations prosecuted by the U.S. military, from major state-on-state conflict to humanitarian operations. However, we anticipate that with the growing reliance of U.S. adversaries, including China, Iran, and Russia, on using disinformation as an indispensable tool of statecraft, and based on the immense volume and array of targets for Russian disinformation in the Ukrainian war, disinformation will continue to be a critical weapon in future warfare.

---

[1] See Jakub Kalenský and Roman Osadchuk, *How Ukraine Fights Russian Disinformation: Beehive vs Mammoth*, Hybrid CoE Research Report 11, Hybrid CoE, January 24, 2024; Adam Fivenson, Galyna Petrenko, Veronika Vichova, and Andrej Poescuk, *Shielding Democracy: Civil Society Adaptations to Kremlin Disinformation About Ukraine*, National Endowment for Democracy, November 9, 2023; JD Maddox, Casi Gentzel, and Adela Levis, "Toward a Whole of Society Framework for Countering Disinformation," Modern War Institute, May 10, 2021; and Iryna Adam, Samantha Lai, Arthur Nelson, Alicia Wanless, and Kamya Yadav, "Emergency Management and Information Integrity: A Framework for Crisis Response," webpage, Carnegie Endowment for International Peace, November 9, 2023.

The lessons we offer are the following, which are summarized in greater detail in the remainder of this chapter:

- Prepare for three theaters of information war.
- Build critical institutions in advance of and during conflict.
- Invest in and work with civil society.
- Build and maintain U.S. institutions critical to countering disinformation during conflict.
- Build and maintain trust.
- Work with and empower local civilian and military influencers.
- Build the resilience of U.S. troops.
- Do not allow coordination to sacrifice speed in responding.
- Be prepared to take risks.
- Plan on resourcing and implementing three critical counterdisinformation tools: debunking, prebunking, and narratives.
- Recognize the risk of waning support over time.

Prepare for Three Theaters of Information War

The expansive nature of Russian propaganda and disinformation that targets not only Ukrainians but also Russians and international communities represents a critical challenge against which the United States must clearly prepare to respond. Several key lessons emerge related to the three theaters of the information war the United States is likely to face in a future conflict.

First, Ukraine's information war has shown how difficult it is to influence audiences that reside in totalitarian states where the government can not only restrict population access to external sources of information but fill that space with its own narrative and implement coercive controls over the population's freedom of expression. Ukraine's inability to influence the Russian population and affect Russia's strategic calculus has been catastrophic, as Russia not only has been able to continue its campaign in Ukraine but can do so seemingly impervious to potential domestic impacts of its own high casualty rates.

The international theater of operations has presented its own challenges as well. First, Russia seems to have initially successfully reached audiences in places like Africa, India, and Latin America. Though Ukrainian organizations have worked to counter disinformation in such places, the efforts seem too few and too limited to have significant impact and overcome Russia's gains and its "first mover" advantage. The most critical audiences for Ukraine, however, remain in Europe and the United States, from which it has received the vast majority of its funding. By almost any count, the Ukrainian narrative has been a resounding success, generating not only sympathy but needed money and military training and equipment. But here the challenge is longevity and overcoming not only organic reluctance of some political actors in the West to provide open-ended support for Ukraine but also Russian disinformation themes that seek to target such actors and accentuate their reluctance. This study did not focus on or analyze international efforts to support Ukraine's information war, but it is clear that such efforts are important to support and reinforce Ukrainian outreach.

Even in Ukraine, the information war is not homogeneous, with Russia paying special attention to influencing audiences near the front lines. This has required Ukraine to go beyond highlighting general Russian disinformation narratives, often posted on civil society websites, and toward identifying the unique themes targeting specific communities and then conducting outreach efforts to communicate to those specific communities and build the capacity of local leadership to identify and respond to Russian disinformation. We can expect future adversaries to conduct similar types of campaigns that complement locally based military operations.

The clear lesson for the United States to consider is the need to plan for three distinct theaters of information war in preparation for a future conflict, with each theater presenting distinctive challenges. It will be critical for the United States to either consider innovative ways to reach and communicate with domestic audiences inside authoritarian countries like Russia or China in the event of an attack on Taiwan, or cede the victory in this theater of information war. The U.S. and international community must likewise rally to more effectively identify, debunk, and prebunk adversary campaigns targeting the rest of the world and work to support a broader array of international civil society organizations that are able to reach critical audiences. U.S. planners must likewise be prepared to confront a diverse and hyperlocal disinformation campaign in the theater of war and ensure that the United States dedicates resources to monitoring such communities and building ties with institutions (civil society and government) that can credibly speak to resident populations.

Build At-Risk Nations' Critical Institutions in Advance of and During Conflict

Build At-Risk Nations' Institutions in Advance of Conflict

One of the central and oft-mentioned lessons of the war in Ukraine is the value of long-term preparation.[2] As highlighted above, preparation for the ensuing Russian invasion in 2022 began as early as 2014. Civil society organizations were created and fully operational, the government implemented key communication structures, and the networks between the two were established. The populace had also been exposed to media literacy education efforts that likely proved critical to the populace's resilience. A representative of the CSC observed that when the Russians attacked, "everyone was in panic," and it would have been impossible to build the infrastructure and the requisite trust among and between institutions at that late stage.[3] A strategic communications adviser agreed, stating,

> This is one of the key lessons from Ukrainian experience, that model should exist before day zero and we should set up formal cooperation between civil society, media and government and they do things together and apply strategies together aimed at building society resilience and more.[4]

A strategic communications adviser who was on the front line of Ukraine's information defense before the war and actively involved in gov-

---

[2] Adam et al., 2023.

[3] Representatives of the CSC, interview with the authors, Kyiv, Ukraine, October 25, 2023.

[4] Strategic adviser at International Media Support, phone interview with the authors, June 27, 2023.

ernment communications since day one of the invasion emphasized that to prepare, the government can

> draw similarities from the corporate world. How the military usually prepares—doing training. We have to do the same—prepare, train, have a department on psyops long before the conflict happens—you have people, you have important channels (YouTube). You have film crews on standby, similar to how your air defense systems are on standby. When the siren is on, I am the speaker, you are the writer, we publish and comment.[5]

Consequently, the United States and allied governments should look to identify key countries at risk for conflict early, be they the Baltic nations that sit on Russia's doorstep in Eastern Europe or Taiwan. The goal, as in Ukraine, is a civil society and government that have the necessary skills and resources to identify and counter foreign disinformation and the interconnections to coordinate such efforts to the extent feasible. Likewise, efforts should be undertaken to build populations' media literacy skills so that they are able to identify and discount adversary disinformation narratives.

Be Prepared to Build the Capacity of Key Institutions During Conflict

Often host nation (i.e., the nation in which the war is taking place) capacity for countering disinformation is consolidated in central government institutions or civil society organizations located within the capital region or other major cities. However, as the Ukraine case study suggests, effectively addressing adversary disinformation must take place in outlying areas or in locales, far from a nation's capital or major cities, that are just as likely to be targeted and critically affected by conflict. The CSC recognized, for example, that Russia has placed a special focus on frontline communities throughout its disinformation campaign. Many local leaders and organizations in such areas have enormous influence and credibility with at-risk populations but have little training or experience in counterdisinformation

---

[5] Strategic communication advisers, interview with the authors, Kyiv, Ukraine, October 25, 2023.

or strategic messaging. Consequently, the CSC has implemented a program to host training programs in such regions that seek to train local leaders and organizations to monitor and recognize Russian disinformation narratives, to respond to such narratives effectively, and to more proactively communicate with the local population. Beyond building local capacity, the program has also helped develop connections between central and outlying government institutions, which has enabled a freer flow of information and intelligence between them.

The lesson here is a relatively basic one. In future contingency operations, the U.S. military and State Department will need to closely consider adversary targets for propaganda and disinformation and evaluate the ability of localized institutions, be they government or civil society, to effectively respond. Where needed, the United States should work with host nation experts to conduct trainings and buttress the capacity of these local institutions.

Invest in and Work with Civil Society

Above we highlight the unique contributions and role of civil society. In addressing the risk of disinformation in future conflict, the United States and its partners will have a variety of choices regarding the institutions they lean on to respond most effectively. The U.S. military and State Department, for example, could fill their own ranks to develop strategic communication and counterdisinformation cells, as well as fund major outside contractors to assist in this work. However, the Ukraine experience highlights the critical role of civil society in serving as a force multiplier for countering a diverse and multifaceted Russian disinformation campaign across all three theaters. A representative of the CSC observed that the biggest success of the CSC is "working with the civil society. . . . It was an idea of the whole society response from day one. We saw civil society as our biggest partner."[6]

Respondents interviewed for this report highlighted a variety of reasons for building up and leaning on civil society to counter disinformation during conflict. The first and maybe most important reason for doing so is

---

[6] Representatives of the CSC, interview with the authors, Kyiv, Ukraine, October 25, 2023.

trust. If the primary goal of such a campaign is to help counter disinformation targeting host nation personnel and ensure society's will to fight, then the trust that society has in any counterdisinformation initiative is critical. If civil society organizations are sufficiently mature and developed, then these organizations will have established relationships with the population likely to make efforts to debunk or prebunk adversary disinformation and promote critical narratives more credible. Established relationships between the civil society and government institutions are also likely to be critical for success, as they will provide the requisite trust for partnerships and collaboration.[7] This trust will also prove critical in addressing domestic cleavages that can be leveraged to bolster disinformation campaigns, especially when the targets of that disinformation may not trust the government or intervening forces. Observed a representative from the National Endowment for Democracy, "Civil society may be better positioned to respond to disinformation internally. The government might not be willing to police information internally. The idea of the government moderating or indicating acceptable speech is controversial."[8] The National Endowment for Democracy representative also highlighted the continuity value of civil society that provides a hedge against government turnover. *"First of all, civil society exists across the governments. If the government changes, if there is a revolution or any change of government, the civil society still exists across the political transitions."*[9]

It is also clearly evident from Ukraine that the task of countering the onslaught of Russian disinformation is just too great for any one institution or organization. Civil society organizations each have their own constituencies and are better attuned to those different audiences and are better able to reach them.[10] More institutions can also better respond to the quantity of adversary propaganda. As one interview participant noted, "Russia spends an enormous number of resources for spreading disinformation in Ukraine and abroad.

---

[7] Representatives of the CSC, interview with the authors, Kyiv, Ukraine, October 25, 2023.

[8] Representative of the National Endowment for Democracy, phone interview with the authors, November 3, 2023.

[9] Representative of the National Endowment for Democracy, phone interview with the authors, November 3, 2023.

[10] Strategic adviser at International Media Support, phone interview with the authors, June 27, 2023.

That's why the more people are involved in countering this information, the better response we can create to it."[11] Adaptation is also key. As one interviewee noted, the "beehive response" is "more flexible and allows for quicker adaptation." Civil society is also able to marshal more expertise, especially in technical areas of media monitoring.[12]

Ultimately, this observation means that it will be critical for the United States to not only invest in building civil society organizations in advance of future conflict but also support and be willing to work closely with such institutions when conflict does arise. It should also take a lesson from the CSC and work to develop U.S. and host nation institutions that can work with and leverage the activities of civil society.

Build and Maintain U.S. Institutions Critical to Countering Disinformation

The United States must also work to build and maintain its own capability for countering foreign disinformation. This study did not undertake a comprehensive analysis of the U.S. government, civilian and military architecture and plans for countering disinformation during conflict, and it seems that no publicly available efforts by other scholars have addressed this issue to date. However, it seems apparent that such an analysis will be critical to identifying the specific steps that the United States must take to prepare for this particular information threat during future conflict. It does appear, though, that U.S. military doctrine is lacking on this specific issue. In a brief review of Department of Defense (DoD) doctrine, Army Field Manual (FM) 3-61, *Communication Strategy and Public Affairs Operations*, offers the most significant treatment of the counterdisinformation topic, providing an entire chapter on countering mis- and disinformation as well as a dedicated appendix that reflects the lead role that public affairs professionals in the Army are likely to play in countering disinformation, per Army Doctrine Publication (ADP)

---

[11] Representative of the VoxUkraine, interview with the authors, Kyiv, Ukraine, October 24, 2023.

[12] Representative of the CSC, interview with the authors, Kyiv, Ukraine, October 25, 2023.

3-13, *Information*.[13] Other U.S. military doctrine makes frequent mention of disinformation but does not offer a specific framework for steps needed to counter it.[14] It will likely be important for future doctrine, particularly that for joint operations, to catch up to the same level of detail offered in FM 3-61. Efforts to counter multimodal and high-volume adversary disinformation during conflict should be a focus of future DoD and interagency training initiatives as well as wargames in order to inform this future doctrine.

It is also worth highlighting two other institutions key to countering foreign disinformation during conflict. First, the State Department's Global Engagement Center (GEC) is tasked with the mission to

> direct, lead, synchronize, integrate, and coordinate U.S. Federal Government efforts to recognize, understand, expose, and counter foreign state and non-state propaganda and disinformation efforts aimed at undermining or influencing the policies, security, or stability of the United States, its allies, and partner nations.[15]

Its work focuses on countering Russian, Iranian, Chinese, and terrorist disinformation campaigns, and it has taken among its key tasks activities to support U.S. allies and overseas civil society organizations directly confronting foreign propaganda. The GEC would likely play a critical role in shaping allied counterdisinformation during future conflict as well as coordinating interagency responses before and during that conflict.

The U.S. Army's psychological operations forces, as well as similar outfits for other services, will also play a critical role in conducting military information support operations. FM 3-61 notes that such operations "help PA [public affairs] personnel to counter adversary efforts of misinformation and disinformation." Such units will play a critical role developing messaging

---

[13] FM 3-61, *Communication Strategy and Public Affairs Operations*, Department of the Army, February 2022; ADP 3-13, *Information*, Department of the Army, November 2023.

[14] Reviewed doctrine includes ADP 3-13, 2023; FM 3-53, *Military Information Support Operations*, Department of the Army, January 2013; Marine Corps Doctrine Publication 8, *Information*, Department of the Navy, June 2022; Joint Publication 3-04, *Information in Joint Operations*, Joint Staff, September 14, 2022; and Joint Publication 3-61, *Public Affairs*, Joint Staff, November 2015 (incorporating Change 1, August 19, 2016).

[15] Global Engagement Center, "Mission and Vision," webpage, U.S Department of State, undated.

series and products that not only counter adversary disinformation but promote narratives that can effectively protect against adversary disinformation. These potential efforts are discussed in greater detail in a subsequent section focused on debunking, prebunking, and narratives.[16]

Recent reports, however, suggest that both the GEC and the Army's psychological operations forces face the risk of near-term funding cuts, perhaps even to the level of an "existential threat."[17] Suffice it to say, such cuts could decrease U.S. capacity to counter adversary disinformation that could undermine core U.S. warfighting advantages in a range of future conflicts, including a war with China.

Build and Maintain Trust

The centrality of trust is its own lesson from the Ukrainian conflict. After the 2022 Russian invasion, Ukrainian society banded together against a common enemy, and trust in the government reached pinnacle levels. This level of trust in the Ukrainian government and mutual antipathy toward invading forces allowed government and civil society efforts to effectively counter Russian disinformation. For example, it was noted how, following the Russian invasion, the Ukrainian "narrative" became consolidated in a "zone of consensus." There were no longer multiple interpretations of what happened but rather "one shared vision." Such a "zone of consensus" may not always be present during U.S. contingency operations, and the lack of trust and unity may prove a significant challenge in countering adversary disinformation.[18]

Whatever trust does exist in operational theaters should not be squandered. To this point Ukrainians urge the use of transparent and honest government and civil society communications. Strategic communication experts highlighted that honest and aboveboard communications have been

---

[16] FM 3-61, 2022.

[17] See Steven Lee Myers, "State Dept.'s Fight Against Disinformation Comes Under Attack," *New York Times*, December 14, 2023; and Cole Livieratos, "Cutting Army Special Operations Will Erode the Military's Ability to Influence the Modern Battlefield," *War on the Rocks*, January 9, 2024.

[18] Strategic adviser at International Media Support, phone interview with the authors, June 27, 2023.

critical for Ukraine.[19] Governments have a variety of tools at their disposal to promote their narrative or counter foreign disinformation, and some of these tools fall into a bucket—often referred to as black public relations—involving efforts that provide fabricated content. Examples include so-called astroturf campaigns, which attempt to fake popular opinion with the use of covertly managed social media accounts.[20] Several respondents interviewed for this report specifically eschewed such influence attempts. Strategic communications experts observed in a joint interview that,

> in the corporate world, [there is] a black and a civilized PR [public relations]. If you want to win the war, you cannot rely on [black communications]. Even brainwashed people have some critical thinking. For how long can you manage the risks [from doing black communications]? One day, you'll get [your campaign outed on] WikiLeaks. This is our value—truth.[21]

They continued, "We need to believe that truth is powerful. Strong people rely on truth; weak people rely on [fabricated content]."[22] Referring to the use of fake astroturf accounts, a CSC representative observed that for a democratic society, "the benefits do not outweigh the risks."[23]

Building and maintaining trust will also be critical for the U.S. government and its military to achieve at home. The United States has been wracked with partisan divisions, and public trust in the U.S. military is at its lowest level in almost two decades.[24] This lack of trust can significantly undermine

---

[19] Strategic communication advisers, interview with the authors, Kyiv, Ukraine, October 25, 2023.

[20] Adam Silverman, "Thinking Security: Black Psyops, Laundering Misinformation, Disinformation, & Agitprop," Ark Valley Voice, November 30, 2019.

[21] Strategic communication advisers, interview with the authors, Kyiv, Ukraine, October 25, 2023.

[22] Strategic communication advisers, interview with the authors, Kyiv, Ukraine, October 25, 2023.

[23] Representatives of the CSC, interview with the authors, Kyiv, Ukraine, October 25, 2023.

[24] Mohamed Younis, "Confidence in U.S. Military Lowest in over Two Decades," Gallup, July 31, 2023.

the success of future military operations. Further, it poses a significant vulnerability to adversary disinformation efforts, as Russia has made it a hallmark of its propaganda efforts to further inflame such tensions. Clearly, the U.S. government and civil society organizations should work to address the potential for basic trust deficits to diminish the ability of the U.S. government to effectively communicate national security priorities to the American public. The U.S. military will also need to take extra care in its operations to ensure its pronouncements and actions during contingency operations maintain trust with the U.S. public, and ensure that its personnel are less susceptible to disinformation, particularly where such messaging leverages preexisting partisan fault lines to its advantage. And to the extent feasible, efforts should be made by planners and research organizations to game out how such challenges could be exploited by adversaries during conflict.

Work with and Empower Local Civilian and Military Influencers

Social media posts generated by wide swaths of Ukrainian society played a critical role in building international support for Ukraine and establishing a groundswell of support that may have helped defend against Russia's internationally focused disinformation campaign. This support was not limited to the response of Ukrainian civilians, in that Ukraine's military personnel also actively shared content from the war's front lines. Early in the war, Ukrainian authorities and civil society actors helped shape the dissemination of this content. Civil society actors helped enlist civilians to promote bands of resistance using online comments to reach and influence Russian citizens and enlisted others to use Twitter and TikTok to communicate with the West. The military also offered broad guidelines for how troops could safely navigate the dangers of the online space but also allowed frontline personnel to use social media.

Such online influencers offered a host of advantages to Ukraine. It allowed the government to leverage the preestablished credibility of these individual influencers, while also enabling them to build relationships with Western audiences by drawing on their own organic creativity, rather than just the formal efforts of government voices.

The U.S. military and broader U.S. government should strategically seek to promote such online voices to help support U.S. national security objectives. Indeed, past work has supported similar recommendations in other settings. For example, Elizabeth Bodine-Baron, Todd C. Helmus, and colleagues argued in 2016 that the United States should work to harness what was a growing online chorus in the Middle East voicing opposition to the actions of the terrorist group the Islamic State. Drawing on a model of influencer communications frequently used in commercial marketing, the authors argued that the United States should work to identify anti–Islamic State influencers on Twitter, engage and build relationships with such personnel to enlist their cooperation, and work to build their capacity by offering training in online outreach and influence and providing access to shareable content such as raw footage that influencers may be interested in disseminating to their audiences.[25] In a subsequent article published on the issue, Helmus argued that the U.S. military should "not only encourage but empower soldiers, sailors, airmen and marines to tell their stories of service on social media."[26]

Build the Resilience of U.S. Troops

Frontline troops in Ukraine have been a persistent target of Russian disinformation narratives, with Russian content highlighting the futility of resistance and urging soldiers to surrender. Russia has also sought to undermine the trust of Ukrainian military personnel for their commanders. Ukraine has responded by working to build up the resilience of its troops through media literacy training and education on how to behave online.

The United States can expect its military personnel to continue to be a target of adversary disinformation, as it has been already. Currently the U.S. military does not provide a mandatory training regimen to promote media literacy. It does offer the 90-minute computer-based Joint Knowledge

---

[25] Elizabeth Bodine-Baron, Todd C. Helmus, Madeline Magnuson, and Zev Winkelman, *Examining ISIS Support and Opposition Networks on Twitter*, RAND, RR-1328-RC, 2016.

[26] Helmus, 2023.

Online course J3ST-US1396, Influence Awareness. This course seeks in part to prepare military personnel to "recognize influence attempts" and gain awareness of adversary influence campaigns.[27] However, the course has been described as "prefabricated and inflexible," and the content addressing promulgation of media literacy skills as "underdeveloped." Most significantly, it is not mandatory; hence, large audiences in DoD likely remain unprotected.[28]

The threat that social media influence campaigns pose to U.S. forces was highlighted in a recent study by the NATO Strategic Communications Center of Excellence (StratCom COE), which conducted an exercise to test the ability of adversaries to collect open-source intelligence on NATO operations. In coordination with NATO, StratCom COE created fake "honeypot" pages and groups on Facebook that looked as if they were associated with an ongoing NATO military exercise. They also created profiles that appeared to impersonate NATO military personnel. They then used Facebook's targeted advertising feature to promote their fake Facebook pages and groups and used the newly created fake accounts to pepper service personnel about their units and operations. They also friended identified service members and used Facebook's friend recommendation algorithm to friend additional contacts. They also identified the Instagram and Twitter accounts belonging to their list of military personnel and analyzed those feeds for intelligence.[29] The research team for the StratCom COE reported that they were able to identify 150 military participants in the exercise and pinpoint the locations of several battalions, including high-value units, as well as collect phone numbers, email addresses, and pictures of equipment from "all participants targeted using social engineering."[30]

Several commentators have urged DoD to adopt more robust media literacy education. Meghan Fitzpatrick and colleagues argue in the U.S. Army

---

[27] Joint Knowledge Online, *Courseware and Capabilities Catalogue*, January 2024.

[28] Fitzpatrick, Gill, and Giles, 2022.

[29] Issie Lapowski, "NATO Group Catfished Soldiers to Prove a Point About Privacy," *Wired*, February 18, 2019.

[30] Sebastian Bay, Giorgio Bertolin, Nora Biteniece, Edward H. Christie, Anton Dek, Rolf E. Fredheim, John D. Gallacher, Kateryna Kononova, and Tetiana Marchenko, *Responding to Cognitive Security Challenges*, NATO StratCom COE, January 2019, p. 13.

War College quarterly, *Parameters*, that the U.S. military "remains unprepared for the way that" adversaries target troops with disinformation in the "internet era" and urge DoD to partner with "public-sector media literacy leaders to develop a dynamic in-person training program."[31] Referring to foreign disinformation and propaganda, Peter Singer and Eric Johnson argue that "every minute of every day, men and women in uniform are attacked by a weapon that threatens them, their services, and the nation. Yet the U.S. military has not trained them to prepare for this onslaught." They state that "digital literacy is a necessary capability" for today's force.[32] Finally, a recent RAND report by Elina Treyger and colleagues urged that the U.S. Air Force and the joint force "should train troops and their family members to expect and recognize disinformation and other information manipulation by Russian actors."[33]

Do Not Allow Coordination to Sacrifice Speed in Responding

Ukraine also offers a complex set of lessons on the value and limits of coordination. Clearly, Ukraine's government institutions have failed to coordinate with one another on messaging activities. And yet the effects of this lack of coordination have not been as catastrophic as imaginable, with the resulting "beehive" approach to counter disinformation seeming to generative positive outcomes for Ukraine's attempts to counter disinformation within its own borders and promote its narrative abroad. The model, however, is not ideal from a unified messaging perspective. The Ukrainian government ostensibly has an official One Voice policy that seeks to promote a unified Ukrainian message, although such a policy was rarely mentioned during the research team's visit to Kyiv. The MoD does

---

[31] Fitzpatrick, Gill, and Giles, 2022.

[32] Peter W. Singer and Eric B. Johnson, "The Need to Inoculate Military Service Members Against Information Threats: The Case for Digital Literacy Training for the Force," *War on the Rocks*, February 1, 2021.

[33] Elina Treyger, Joe Cheravitch, and Raphael S. Cohen, *Russian Disinformation Efforts on Social Media*, RAND, RR-4373/2-AF, 2022.

implement measures to coordinate its communication efforts, but it also allows a bottom-up approach to communications, with brigades and squads allowed, in the words of one report, "vast leeway" to communicate messages. And the ministry leans on what seem to be independent social media posts disseminated by frontline personnel.[34]

The same issues confront Ukraine's civil society. Here, multiple organizations compete for limited dollars and efforts frequently overlap, such as the numerous initiatives to monitor Telegram. The NDI Disinformation Coordination Hub is the major pathway for coordinating civil society efforts, and it likely helps coordinate a group of independent civil society actors as well as it can.

Altogether, Ukraine's experience suggests that one potential lesson for countering disinformation operations in a future conflict may be on the limits of coordinating such messaging campaigns in the first place. It may be wise to coordinate major government communication campaigns that reach domestic and international audiences, and it is clearly ideal to foster collaborative relationships and mechanisms within and across different state institutions. However, countering foreign disinformation, particularly during a conflict, may also require a loosely coordinated, network-based response. With Russia producing a rapid and high-volume disinformation campaign that draws on a multitude of potential communication channels that reach different segments of Ukrainian society (there are at least 100 channels on Telegram dedicated to Ukrainian audiences, for example), loose coordination and built-in redundancies may enable rapid detection and responses to the most damaging narratives.[35]

---

[34] Ekman and Nilsson, 2023.

[35] Some in DoD speak of developing a "common operational picture" for media monitoring that would, for example, enable a signal display or analysis of the country's media picture and, presumably, adversary disinformation narratives. However, in Ukraine, Russia's full-throated disinformation campaign that exploits multiple media channels with a high volume of content likely precludes any single common operational picture. This is particularly tricky for Telegram, which has over 100 separate channels dedicated to Ukraine. There is also Facebook, Twitter, and VK, as well as Russian overt and more covert news websites. Anastasiia Shevchenko, "Mapping of Telegram Channels in Ukraine, a Year into the Full-Scale War," *The Fix*, April 21, 2023.

Summing up the Ukrainian experience, a representative of the Atlantic Council's Digital Forensic Research Lab, who is based in Kyiv, observes,

> There is no ideal architecture. We have here a multitude of actors that overlap. But it is better to overreact. It is not a problem from a Ukrainian perspective. If there are two debunks or three different organizations debunking something, it is better than nothing. Repetitiveness is not bad. From the perspective of limited resources, it might be. But not in this case.[36]

Jakub Kalenský and Roman Osadchuk, in their wrap-up of ten lessons from Ukraine for countering disinformation, write similarly that "more actors working on the same topic means more reliable output, faster responses, and safeguards against the failure of one of them. In coordination, the loose nature and lack of formal procedures facilitates and speeds up responses."[37] To this end, the United States need not pursue an elusive, highly efficient, and well-apportioned response to monitoring and coordinating a response to disinformation in place of an inefficient but redundant one that enables better, faster, and more attuned outreach to specific audiences.

Be Prepared to Take Risks

A major factor underlying the success of Ukrainian communication efforts, particularly those targeting international audiences, was the country's willingness to take risks. This is most aptly seen in the Ukrainian MoD's Twitter account. The MoD not only enlisted private-sector and civil society entities to manage and run the account, but the account's success has been linked to its ability to make use of sometimes irreverent humor. Commenting on this account, but also more broadly on the government's partnership with civil society, a strategic communications expert who supported the

---

[36] Representative of the Atlantic Council's Digital Forensic Research Lab, interview with the authors, Kyiv, Ukraine, October 25, 2023.

[37] Kalenský and Osadchuk, 2024; Fivenson et al., 2023.

MoD Twitter account observed, "Ukraine was successful from the very beginning by telling a truly diverse story. Ukraine had humor, tragedy, pain, love, beauty, not just a story of terrible pain."[38] Ukrainian society "gave the Ukrainian government this creativity, innovation, everything that shapes Ukraine's resistance in the eyes of foreigners." In speaking to the country's reliance on local influencers, one journalist commented that "only the most engaging content—the funniest, the most heart-rending, the most shocking—can hope to reach a wider audience."[39]

Risk, however, is not the forte of U.S. government communication efforts. Recent RAND research, for example, highlighted how U.S. bureaucracies have often feared that taking risks critical to effective public communications could backfire, given that a single mistake could quickly be highlighted by U.S. news organizations.[40] Within the Department of State, the GEC and its predecessor, the Center for Strategic Counterterrorism Communications, have both been subject to numerous media exposés, and the Center for Strategic Counterterrorism Communications was ultimately shuttered in part because one of its videos was ridiculed by John Oliver on his HBO talk show *Last Week Tonight*.[41] The DoD Office of Strategic Influence, developed shortly after September 11, 2001, in order to counter jihadi ideology, was shuttered due to similar publicity.[42] The result of such concerns over risk is that senior government leaders and military commanders often implement cumbersome approval processes that slow response times and are emblematic of a reluctance to take risks in implementing programs

---

[38] Strategic communications expert, interview with the authors, Kyiv, Ukraine, October 24, 2023.

[39] York, 2023.

[40] Linda Robinson, Todd C. Helmus, Raphael S. Cohen, Alireza Nader, Andrew Radin, Madeline Magnuson, and Katya Migacheva, *Modern Political Warfare: Current Practices and Possible Response*, RAND, RR-1772-A, 2018.

[41] Helene Cooper, "U.S. Drops Snark in Favor of Emotion to Undercut Extremists," *New York Times*, July 28, 2016; Greg Miller, "Panel Casts Doubt Against U.S. Propaganda Efforts Against ISIS," *Washington Post*, December 2, 2015; Jacob Silverman, "That Propaganda Program Bill Clinton Praised Hillary For? It Was Considered a Failure," *Politico*, July 27, 2016.

[42] Pamela Hess, "DOD to Close 'Influence' Office," UPI, February 26, 2002.

that can effectively speak to critical audiences. The same RAND report subsequently urged,

> Senior leaders must not just empower but also *encourage* subordinates to accept risk. With the development of effective and speedy processes for approving products, it is critical that communicators take reasonable risks in the pursuit of success. . . . With this risk-taking, mistakes will happen; and a press, fascinated by propaganda, will take notice. Senior leaders, especially within the White House, must be willing to provide the necessary political cover to the bureaucracy, modify plans and operations accordingly, and push on.[43]

Plan on Resourcing and Implementing Three Critical Tools: Debunking, Prebunking, and Narratives

Lessons from Ukraine's information war suggest that debunking, prebunking, and the promulgation of proactive information narratives will prove critical tools to countering and mitigating the impact of adversary disinformation. Overall, the U.S. Department of State as well as the U.S. military will need to ensure that these three approaches are effectively resourced, implemented, and integrated in military theaters of operation.

Debunking

Debunking refers to offering and publicizing corrections to false information after that false information has been released. It is evident from the previous review of Ukraine's counterdisinformation operations that debunking emerging Russian disinformation is an oft-used tool. Civil society organizations including VoxUkraine and StopFake, as well as the government institutions of the CSC and the CCD, engage in their own efforts to monitor common channels for Russian disinformation, identify emerging false content, and then, if such content appears particularly damaging or is gaining

---

[43] Robinson et al., 2018, pp. 260, 261.

initial traction on social media, offer a correction of the false content. These corrections are often posted to civil society websites but, if warranted, are disseminated more proactively via ministry spokespersons and television and radio channels that can reach larger targeted audiences. In a particularly critical program, both VoxUkraine and StopFake highlight false stories circulating on Facebook, which then posts a warning label on the content and reduces its circulation on the platform. Although some have critiqued the efficacy of fact-checking labels, research overall has borne out evidence of their effectiveness. Summative studies, which examine the overall effect of some intervention observed in a large body of research, show, for example, that real-time corrections, crowdsourced fact checking, and algorithmic tagging do mitigate the effects of false information.[44] While such mitigation is often less pronounced among those who are the most politically biased in favor of the content, this evidence suggests that the positive effects of such interventions are still strong. One drawback of debunking efforts is that they risk publicizing the disinformation to audiences that would not otherwise receive the message, so care must be taken to only debunk narratives that risk going viral.

Prebunking

Prebunking also represents a critical tool. This approach, alternatively referred to as an inoculation treatment, seeks to help audiences "develop psychological resilience to disinformation before they ever encounter misleading claims," per the words of Yasmin Green, the CEO of Google's "think-do" tank Jigsaw.[45] The goal of prebunking is to protect audiences against persuasion attempts by presenting a weakened form of those persuasive arguments much in the same way that vaccines confer protection by introducing a weakened form of a virus into the immune system. Inoculation messages confer attitudinal resistance by presenting two key messages. The first is a forewarning of an impending attack on one's attitudes, and the second

---

[44] Walter et al., 2021.

[45] Yasmin Green, "Disinformation as a Weapon of War: The Case for Prebunking," webpage, Friends of Europe, December 12, 2022.

is "raising and refuting counterarguments,"[46] or exposing individuals to a "weakened (micro)dose of misinformation that contains a preemptive refutation (or prebunk) of the anticipated misleading arguments or persuasion techniques."[47]

Overall, inoculation and prebunking strategies have proved effective. A number of studies have evaluated the efficacy of inoculation interventions. A 2010 meta-analysis of 54 studies testing the efficacy of inoculation interventions demonstrated that health inoculation messages were more effective than both supportive messages and no treatment controls in conferring resistance to persuasive messages.[48] It also demonstrated that inoculation messages were effective even when outcomes were tested on misinformation not addressed in the original intervention. For example, Jon Roozenbeek and colleagues developed five 90-second videos that conveyed a forewarning and preemptive refutation of five different types of manipulation techniques: emotionally manipulative language, incoherence, false dichotomies, scapegoating, and ad hominem attacks.[49] In testing with a randomized control trial, all five videos were shown to significantly improve the quality of participant sharing decisions and increase discernment between manipulative and nonmanipulative content.

One critical example of prebunking in the war in Ukraine is the U.S. effort to release intelligence of Russia's impending false flag operation, which would otherwise have offered a false justification for invasion of Ukraine as an act of Russian self-defense. This release of sensitive intelligence, which surely required significant bureaucratic coordination to execute, highlighted in very specific ways how Russia planned to fake a

---

[46] Josh Compton, Ben Jackson, and James A. Dimmock, "Persuading Others to Avoid Persuasion: Inoculation Theory and Resistant Health Attitudes," *Frontiers in Psychology*, Vol. 9, No. 7, February 9, 2016.

[47] Jon Roozenbeek, Sander van der Linden, Beth Goldberg, Steve Rathje, and Stephan Lewandowsky, "Psychological Inoculation Improves Resilience Against Misinformation on Social Media," *Science Advances*, Vol. 8, No. 34, August 24, 2022.

[48] John A. Banas and Stephen A. Rains, "A Meta-Analysis of Research on Inoculation Theory," *Communication Monographs*, Vol. 77, No. 3, 2010.

[49] Roozenbeek et al., 2022.

Ukrainian attack. It was so well timed that the planned Russian operation was reportedly aborted. And even if the Russians had proceeded with such an operation, the prebunk would have almost certainly limited its persuasive appeal. The Ukrainian government and civil society have also worked similarly to prebunk Russian propaganda, releasing information to the Ukrainian and international public when warranted by Russia's assessed next steps.

It also been suggested that debunks offer their own prebunking value as Russian attempts to recycle false information meet resistance among the population, which has already been exposed to the falsified narrative. Even Google helped to counter Russian disinformation as it helped fund an initiative that shared video content prebunking common Russian narratives that attempted to scapegoat Ukrainian refugees in Europe. Highlighting the importance of such nongovernmental efforts, this initiative ultimately reached a quarter of the Polish population and a third of all Czechs and Slovaks, and surveys suggested an improvement in audience ability to discern Russian propaganda as a result.[50]

Still, prebunking that forewarns audiences about specific adversary narratives is more challenging than debunking merely because it requires advance knowledge of an adversary campaign. "Prebunking is harder," observed one representative of the CCD, who noted that Ukraine can "see when Russia is starting to do something. We cannot directly forecast, but we feel, in our guts, that something is coming up." The CCD have also seen, for example, that Russians often try to build an "information alibi" before an attack. "When Russians want to bomb a place, for example, Kremenchuk Railway Station, . . . they [will say in advance that] Ukraine was going to do it."[51] The CCD representative also alluded to what is a critical ingredient in prebunking operations: intelligence. And indeed, it was intelligence that enabled the U.S. prebunk of the Russian false flag operation. This points to the critical value of focusing U.S. intelligence on identifying emerging adversary disinformation campaigns and collaborating with strategic communicators to out such campaigns.

---

[50] Green, 2022.

[51] Officials at the CCD, interview with the authors, Kyiv, Ukraine, October 24, 2023.

Proactive Narrative Campaigns

Finally, proactive information campaigns promulgated by the Ukrainians have played a critical role in promoting resilience to Russian propaganda. Scholars Christopher Paul and Miriam Matthews write that foreign disinformation can be "disadvantaged" if audiences are already "primed" with the correct information. They consequently argue that it is important to counter not the adversary propaganda itself but the potential "effects" of that propaganda.[52] A consistent narrative is also likely needed to counter the illusory truth effect, or the cumulative impact that consistently relayed false information can generate over time. If standard debunking efforts are not sufficient to counter this illusory truth effect, then it is critical to also counter it with a compelling and consistent narrative campaign that can effectively compete with the adversary disinformation.

A number of the Ukrainians interviewed for this report agree. As one participant at a meeting of NDI's Disinformation Coordination Hub observed, the question is, "Should we be reactive and respond, or can we promote our own narratives?" For short-term purposes, the participant said debunking is helping. But he also highlighted that Ukrainians "shouldn't just be in the narrative built by Russia, but tell our own story, not starting by 'we are not as bad as Russia says.'"[53] Another civil society representative says, "We should not just debunk. We should have our own narrative—who we are and what we are. And only after that, we can debunk other narratives."[54]

Ukraine achieved this with stunning success on the international level. Pronouncements from President Zelenskyy and the social media posts of Ukrainians, combined of course with their successes on the battlefield, communicated a narrative of Ukrainian resilience that overshadowed subsequent Russian disinformation campaigns. More tactically, Ukraine was able to quickly seize the narrative about Russian atrocities and provide a layer of protection against Russian denials. Even Ukrainian efforts to respond to

---

[52] Paul and Matthews, 2016.

[53] Participants in the NDI Disinformation Coordination Hub, interview with the authors, Kyiv, Ukraine, October 24, 2023.

[54] Representatives of the Ukrainian Prism, interview with the authors, Kyiv, Ukraine, October 25, 2023.

Russia's 2014 invasion of Crimea laid the groundwork for a united response to the second invasion. Observed a strategic communication adviser, "But it was based on the ground we built of preparing the society, building the values. We withstood because we grew and developed a sense of patriotism. When something does happen, people stand up. People grabbed machine guns on the street and were ready to defend."[55]

Recognize the Risk of Waning Support over Time

As we highlighted in our main analysis, online engagement in pro-Ukrainian content has declined since the start of the war, and support for Ukraine in particular regions, especially the United States and select European countries, has similarly declined. Two particular issues may be at play here. The first is the challenge of maintaining international attention on a crisis and the decline of the war's novelty. Videos showing successful Ukrainian attacks against Russian tanks, for example, fascinate audiences at first but become increasingly old hat over time. Second, there may be a risk that Russian disinformation generates cumulative effects over time, a notion consistent with scientific evidence backing what is known as the illusory truth effect. After audiences repeatedly hear the same message, even if disputed, over time it may find ways of sinking in. Consequently, the longer a conflict continues, the more it may favor U.S. adversaries in the information domain. Such forms of waning U.S. influence should be incorporated in wargames and considered as a potential risk to the success of war plans. In such situations, the United States may need to think through more novel forms of messaging that can maintain or generate new attention on the conflict to sustain broader will to fight longer-term conflicts.

---

[55] Strategic communication advisers, interview with the authors, Kyiv, Ukraine, October 25, 2023.

Conclusion

Disinformation is increasingly used as a weapon of war, and nowhere is that more obvious than in the Russian war against Ukraine. As other scholars have highlighted and as we demonstrate in this report, Russia has been engaged in a broad and high-volume effort to sow false narratives designed to promote domestic support for the war, undermine the Ukrainians' will to fight, and chip away at international support for Ukraine. It seems logical that future adversaries will likewise make use of false narratives to enable combat operations and other forms of military operations.

The United States, NATO, and other allies must be prepared to counter such false narratives and must prepare in advance to bolster the capabilities of nations that will serve at the front lines of war. Highlighting ways to accomplish these critical objectives has been the goal of this report. As such, we have reviewed how Russia has sought to use disinformation to counter Ukraine across what we call the three theaters of information war, and we have highlighted the ways in which Ukraine has worked to counter such disinformation narratives.

Based on this analysis, we have identified 11 key lessons that the United States and its allies must learn to prepare for future conflict. We recognize that these lessons may not constitute the full array of lessons and preparations needed to effectively counter disinformation during conflict, and more research into these issues is certainly required. Critical future research should likewise explore lessons from the Israeli war in Gaza, how China may seek to leverage disinformation during conflict, and how nations in China's cross hairs, most prominently Taiwan, are prepared to counter such disinformation. The United States and NATO will also need to make proactive use of wargames, lessons-learned studies, and capability gap analyses to highlight limitations in their own doctrine, organization, training, materiel, leadership and education, personnel, and facilities to counter disinformation in conflict. While we highlight in this report the critical role of building host nation capacity to counter disinformation over time, this research was not designed to offer specific recommendations for how *best* to do so. Consequently, future studies should also assess best practices and best approaches for such capacity-building efforts.

Abbreviations

ADP	Army Doctrine Publication
CCD	Center for Countering Disinformation
COVID-19	coronavirus disease 2019
CSC	Center for Strategic Communications and Information Security
DoD	Department of Defense
EU	European Union
FM	Field Manual
GEC	Global Engagement Center
IREX	International Research and Exchanges Board
MoD	Ukrainian Ministry of Defense
NATO	North Atlantic Treaty Organization
NDI	National Democratic Institute
NGO	nongovernmental organization
StratCom	Strategic Communication Department of the Office of the Commander-in-Chief of the Armed Forces of Ukraine
StratCom COE	NATO Strategic Communications Center of Excellence
VK	VKontakte

References

Abnett, Kate, "EU on Track to Quit Russian Fossil Fuels—Report," Reuters, October 24, 2023.

Adam, Iryna, Samantha Lai, Arthur Nelson, Alicia Wanless, and Kamya Yadav, "Emergency Management and Information Integrity: A Framework for Crisis Response," webpage, Carnegie Endowment for International Peace, November 9, 2023. As of April 16, 2024:
https://carnegieendowment.org/2023/11/09/emergency-management-and
-information-integrity-framework-for-crisis-response-pub-90959

ADP—*See* Army Doctrine Publication.

Armstrong, Martin, "Has Ukraine News Fatigue Set In?" webpage, Statista, August 24, 2022. As of February 15, 2024:
https://www.statista.com/chart/28071/google-news-search-interest-for-ukraine/

Army Doctrine Publication 3-0, *Operations*, Headquarters, Department of the Army, 2017.

Army Doctrine Publication 3-13, *Information*, Department of the Army, November 2023.

Army TV—Ukrainian Military Channel, YouTube, undated. As of February 15, 2024:
https://www.youtube.com/channel/UCWRZ7gEgbry5FI2-46EX3jA

ArmyInform, "What Are You Fighting For?—The Ukrainian Military Has Published an Urgent Appeal to Russian Soldiers" ["За що ви воюєте?— Українські військові опублікували термінове звернення до російських солдатів"], webpage, October 24, 2022. As of June 7, 2024:
https://armyinform.com.ua/2022/10/24/za-shho-vy-voyuyete-ukrayinski
-vijskovi-opublikuvaly-terminove-zvernennya-do-rosijskyh-soldativ/

Atanesian, Grigor, "Russia in Africa: How Disinformation Operations Target the Continent," BBC, February 1, 2023.

Balmforth, Tom, and Filipp Lebedev, "Ukrainian Intercepts Show Russian Soldiers' Anger at Losses, Disarray," Reuters, September 5, 2023.

Banas, John A., and Stephen A. Rains, "A Meta-Analysis of Research on Inoculation Theory," *Communication Monographs*, Vol. 77, No. 3, 2010.

Barnes, Julian E., "U.S. Exposes What It Says Is Russian Effort to Fabricate Pretext for Invasion," *New York Times*, February 3, 2022.

Barnes, Julian E., and Edward Wong, "U.S. and Ukrainian Groups Pierce Putin's Propaganda Bubble," *New York Times*, April 13, 2022.

Bay, Sebastian, Giorgio Bertolin, Nora Biteniece, Edward H. Christie, Anton Dek, Rolf E. Fredheim, John D. Gallacher, Kateryna Kononova, and Tetiana Marchenko, *Responding to Cognitive Security Challenges*, NATO StratCom COE, January 2019. As of September 20, 2021:
https://stratcomcoe.org/pdfjs/?file=/cuploads/pfiles/web_Responing-to
-Cognitive.pdf

Belton, Catherine, and Joseph Menn, "Russian Trolls Target U.S. Support for Ukraine, Kremlin Documents Show," *Washington Post*, April 8, 2024.

Bergengruen, Vera, "Inside the Kremlin's Year of Ukraine Propaganda," *Time*, February 22, 2023.

Bertrand, Natasha, and Jeremy Herb, "First on CNN: US Intelligence Indicates Russia Preparing Operation to Justify Invasion of Ukraine," CNN, January 14, 2022.

Blankenship, Mary, and Aloysius Uche Ordu, "Russian Disinformation in Africa: What's Sticking and What's Not," Brookings, October 17, 2022.

Bodine-Baron, Elizabeth, Todd C. Helmus, Madeline Magnuson, and Zev Winkelman, *Examining ISIS Support and Opposition Networks on Twitter*, RAND, RR-1328-RC, 2016. As of June 7, 2024:
https://www.rand.org/pubs/research_reports/RR1328.html

Bomprezzi, Pietro, Yelmurat Dyussimbinov, André Frank, Ivan Kharitonov, and Christoph Trebesch, "Ukraine Support Tracker," webpage, Kiel Institute for the World Economy, undated. As of February 15, 2024:
https://www.ifw-kiel.de/topics/war-against-ukraine/ukraine-support-tracker

Bond, Shannon, "False Information Is Everywhere. 'Pre-Bunking' Tries to Head It Off Early," NPR, October 28, 2022.

Bradshaw, Samantha, and Philip N. Howard, *The Global Disinformation Order: 2019 Global Inventory of Organized Social Media Manipulation*, University of Oxford, 2019. As of February 14, 2024:
https://demtech.oii.ox.ac.uk/wp-content/uploads/sites/12/2019/09/CyberTroop
-Report19.pdf

Brandt, Jessica, Valerie Wirtschafter, and Adya Danaditya, "Popular Podcasters Spread Russian Disinformation About Ukraine Biolabs," Brookings, March 23, 2022.

Bubola, Emma, "Slovakia's Election Could Echo in Ukraine. Here's What to Expect," *New York Times*, September 30, 2023.

Cerda, Andy, "About Half of Republicans Now Say the U.S. Is Providing Too Much Aid to Ukraine," Pew Research Center, December 8, 2023.

Coleman, Julie, "Russian Operatives Sent 5,000 Text Messages in a Failed Attempt to Incite Ukrainians to Attack Their Own Capitol," *Business Insider*, April 1, 2022.

Compton, Josh, Ben Jackson, and James A. Dimmock, "Persuading Others to Avoid Persuasion: Inoculation Theory and Resistant Health Attitudes," *Frontiers in Psychology*, Vol. 9, No. 7, February 9, 2016.

"Conflict with Ukraine: Assessments for November 2023," webpage, Levada Center, undated. As of March 22, 2024:
https://www.levada.ru/en/tag/ukraine/

Cooper, Helene, "U.S. Drops Snark in Favor of Emotion to Undercut Extremists," *New York Times*, July 28, 2016.

Danishevska, Kateryna, "Russians Spreading Deepfakes with Ukraine's Top Officials: How to Distinguish Lies," RBC-Ukraine, November 8, 2023. As of February 15, 2024:
https://newsukraine.rbc.ua/news/russians-are-spreading-deepfakes-with-ukraine-1699442500.html

Dan'kova, Nataliya, "How 'FreeDom' Works on the Maidan in Russia and Helps Russians Surrender. Discussion at National Media Talk" ["Як 'FreeДом' працює на Майдан у Росії та допомагає росіянам здаватися в полон. Дискусія на National Media Talk"], Detector Media, October 15, 2023. As of June 7, 2024:
https://detector.media/rinok/article/218089/2023-10-15-yak-freedom-pratsyuie-na-maydan-u-rosii-ta-dopomagaie-rosiyanam-zdavatysya-v-polon-dyskusiya-na-national-media-talk/

Defense of Ukraine [@DefenceU], "Artillerymen of the 17th tank brigade of the #UAarmy have opened the holiday season for ruscists. Some bathed in the Siverskyi Donets River, and some were burned by the May sun," Twitter post, May 11, 2022. As of February 15, 2024:
https://twitter.com/DefenceU/status/1524438980191731717

Defense of Ukraine [@DefenceU], "Sophie Marceau . . . Isabelle Adjani . . . Brigitte Bardot . . . Emmanuel Macron! . . . and CAESARs! 🏴󠁮🖤❚❚," Twitter post, October 12, 2022. As of February 20, 2024:
https://twitter.com/DefenceU/status/1580090899228418048

Delegation of the European Union to the United States of America, "EU Assistance to Ukraine (in U.S. Dollars)," webpage, February 22, 2024. As of April 10, 2024:
https://www.eeas.europa.eu/delegations/united-states-america/eu-assistance-ukraine-us-dollars_en?s=253

Demus, Alyssa, Khrystyna Holynska, and Krystyna Marcinek, *The Nightingale Versus the Bear: What Persuasion Research Reveals About Ukraine's and Russia's Messaging on the War*, RAND, RR-A2032-1, 2023. As of February 15, 2024:
https://www.rand.org/pubs/research_reports/RRA2032-1.html

Detector Media, homepage, undated. As of February 15, 2024:
https://en.detector.media

Detector Media, "Media Literacy Index of Ukrainians: 2020–2022," webpage, April 21, 2023. As of February 15, 2024:
https://en.detector.media/post/media-literacy-index-of-ukrainians-2020-2022
-short-presentation

Detector Media, "Tactics and Tools: How Russian Propaganda Uses Corruption in Ukraine to Achieve Its Goals," webpage, August 11, 2023. As of February 15, 2024:
https://disinfo.detector.media/en/post/how-russian-propaganda-uses-corruption
-in-ukraine-to-achieve-its-goals

Dickinson, Peter, "Analysis: Ukraine Bans Kremlin-Linked TV Channels," Atlantic Council, February 5, 2021.

Digital Forensic Research Lab, "In Latin America, Russia's Ambassadors and State Media Tailor Anti-Ukraine Content to the Local Context," Atlantic Council, February 29, 2024. As of April 10, 2024:
https://www.atlanticcouncil.org/in-depth-research-reports/issue-brief/in
-latin-america-russias-ambassadors-and-state-media-tailor-anti-ukraine
-content-to-the-local-context/

Dovidka.info, homepage, undated. As of February 15, 2024:
https://dovidka.info/en/about-us/

Ebert, Niklas, "What's at Stake in the EU Elections: Ukraine Aid," German Marshall Fund of the United States, February 20, 2024.

Ekman, Ivar, and Per-Erik Nilsson, *Ukraine's Information Front: Strategic Communication During Russia's Full-Scale Invasion of Ukraine*, Swedish Armed Forces, April 23, 2023. As of February 15, 2024:
https://foi.se/rest-api/report/FOI-R—5451—SE

Episheva, Anna [@avalaina], "My niece was supposed to graduate this year from her high school . . . ," Twitter post, June 7, 2022. As of February 15, 2024:
https://twitter.com/avalaina/status/1534104594976055305

European Commission, "Europeans Continue to Strongly Support Ukraine, Eurobarometer Shows," webpage, December 13, 2023.

Field Manual 3-53, *Military Information Support Operations*, Department of the Army, January 2013.

Field Manual 3-61, *Communication Strategy and Public Affairs Operations*, Department of the Army, February 2022.

Filter, "National Media Literacy Project," webpage, undated. As of April 16, 2024:
https://filter.mkip.gov.ua/about-the-project/

Fitzpatrick, Meghan, Ritu Gill, and Jennifer F. Giles, "Information Warfare: Lessons in Inoculation to Disinformation," *Parameters: U.S. Army War College Quarterly*, Vol. 52, No. 1, 2022.

Fivenson, Adam, Galyna Petrenko, Veronika Vichova, and Andrej Poescuk, *Shielding Democracy: Civil Society Adaptations to Kremlin Disinformation About Ukraine*, National Endowment for Democracy, November 9, 2023. As of February 15, 2024:
https://www.ned.org/wp-content/uploads/2023/02/NED_FORUM-Shielding-Democracy.pdf

FM—*See* Field Manual.

FreeDom, "About Us," webpage, undated. As of March 22, 2024:
https://uatv.ua/en/about-us/

German Marshall Fund Alliance for Securing Democracy, "ASD Social Data Search," webpage, undated. As of February 15, 2024:
https://securingdemocracy.gmfus.org/asd-social-data-search/?q=Nazi*&country-Russia=true&country-Russia=true&product=%28product+eq+%27Hamilton%27+or+product2+eq+%27Hamilton%27%29&start-date=2022-02-01&end-date=2022-07-31

Gilbert, David, "Russia Can Now Jail People for 15 Years for Tweeting About the War on Ukraine," *Vice*, March 4, 2022.

Global Engagement Center, "Mission and Vision," webpage, U.S Department of State, undated. As of February 15, 2024:
https://www.state.gov/bureaus-offices/under-secretary-for-public-diplomacy-and-public-affairs/global-engagement-center/

Goldsmith, Kristofer, *An Investigation into Foreign Entities Who Are Targeting Servicemembers and Veterans Online*, Vietnam Veterans of America, 2019. As of February 14, 2024:
https://vva.org/wp-content/uploads/2019/09/VVA-Investigation.pdf

Golovchenko, Yevgeniy, "Fighting Propaganda with Censorship: A Study of the Ukrainian Ban on Russian Social Media," *Journal of Politics*, Vol. 84, No. 2, April 2022.

Gordon, Michael R., Gabriele Steinhauser, Dustin Volz, and Ann M. Simmons, "Russian Intelligence Is Pushing False Claims of U.S. Biological Testing in Africa, U.S. Says," *Wall Street Journal*, February 8, 2024.

Gramlich, John, "What Public Opinion Surveys Found in the First Year of the War in Ukraine," Pew Research Center, February 23, 2023.

Green, Yasmin, "Disinformation as a Weapon of War: The Case for Prebunking," webpage, Friends of Europe, December 12, 2022.

Hassan, Aumyo, and Sarah J. Barber, "The Effects of Repetition Frequency on the Illusory Truth Effect," *Cognitive Research: Principles and Implications*, Vol. 6, December 2021.

Helmus, Todd C., "The Ukrainian Army Is Leveraging Online Influencers. Can the U.S. Military?" *War on the Rocks*, March 1, 2023.

Helmus, Todd C., Elizabeth Bodine-Baron, Andrew Radin, Madeline Magnuson, Joshua Mendelsohn, William Marcellino, Andriy Bega, and Zev Winkelman, *Russian Social Media Influence: Understanding Russian Propaganda in Eastern Europe*, RAND, RR-2237-OSD, 2018. As of February 14, 2024: https://www.rand.org/pubs/research_reports/RR2237.html

Helmus, Todd C., and William Marcellino, "Lies, Misinformation Play Key Role in Israel-Hamas Fight," *RAND Blog*, October 31, 2023. As of February 14, 2024: https://www.rand.org/pubs/commentary/2023/10/lies-misinformation-play -key-role-in-israel-hamas-fight.html

Hess, Pamela, "DOD to Close 'Influence' Office," UPI, February 26, 2002. As of July 30, 2016: http://www.upi.com/Business_News/Security-Industry/2002/02/26/DOD-to -close-influence-office/73281014757331/

Hopkins, Valerie, "In Video, a Defiant Zelensky Says, 'We Are Here,'" *New York Times*, February 27, 2022.

"How the Kremlin's Internet Propaganda HQ Operates," *The Bell*, September 27, 2023.

"An Information Brochure 'In Case of an Emergency or War' Was Presented in Kyiv" ["У Києві презентували інформаційну брошуру 'У разі надзвичайної ситуації або війни'"], *Army Inform*, June 23, 2021. As of February 15, 2024: https://armyinform.com.ua/2021/06/23/u-kyyevi-prezentuvaly-informaczijnu -broshuru-u-razi-nadzvychajnoyi-sytuacziyi-abo-vijny/

Institute for Strategic Dialogue, "ISD's Digital Investigation on Syria Disinformation," webpage, July 13, 2022. As of February 14, 2024: https://www.isdglobal.org/digital_dispatches/isds-digital-investigation-on -syria-disinformation/

International Research and Exchanges Board, "Learn to Discern," webpage, undated. As of February 15, 2024: https://www.irex.org/project/learn-discern

International Research and Exchanges Board, "Strengthening Media Literacy in the Ukrainian Education System," webpage, undated. As of February 15, 2024: https://www.irex.org/project/strengthening-media-literacy-ukrainian -education-system

Internews Ukraine, homepage, undated. As of February 15, 2024: https://internews.org/

Internews Ukraine, "Ukrainians Increasingly Rely on Telegram Channels for News and Information During Wartime," webpage, November 1, 2023. As of February 15, 2024: https://internews.org/ukrainians-increasingly-rely-on-telegram-channels-for -news-and-information-during-wartime

Ioffe, Julia [@juliaioffe], "'I'll record this in Russian so it's f—ing clearer,' says this happy (Ukrainian) warrior. 'Guys, you're f—ed,'" Twitter post, February 25, 2022. As of February 15, 2024:
https://twitter.com/juliaioffe/status/1497425699132563457?lang=en

IREX—*See* International Research and Exchanges Board.

I Want to Live, "About the Project 'I Want to Live'" ["О Проекте 'Хочу Жить'"], webpage, undated. As of March 4, 2024:
http://hochuzhit.com/

Joint Knowledge Online, *Courseware and Capabilities Catalogue*, January 2024. As of February 15, 2024:
https://www.jcs.mil/Portals/36/Documents/JKO/JKO_Course_Catalog.pdf?ver
=jy-yABnnNzXvOIvC1bZbUg%3D%3D

Joint Publication 3-04, *Information in Joint Operations*, Joint Staff, September 14, 2022.

Joint Publication 3-61, *Public Affairs*, Joint Staff, November 2015 (incorporating Change 1, August 19, 2016).

Kalenský, Jakub, and Roman Osadchuk, *How Ukraine Fights Russian Disinformation: Beehive vs Mammoth*, Hybrid CoE Research Report 11, Hybrid CoE, January 24, 2024. As of February 15, 2024:
https://www.hybridcoe.fi/wp-content/uploads/2024/01/20240124-Hybrid
-CoE-Research-Report-11-How-UKR-fights-RUS-disinfo-WEB.pdf

Kleinschmidt, Jochen, Artem Miniailo, Rashid Gabdulhakov, and Chelsea Ngoc Minh Nguyen, "Perceptions of Russia's War in the Global South," *Russian Analytical Digest*, Vol. 305, November 30, 2023.

Kramer, Andrew E., "Disinformation Is a Weapon Regularly Deployed in Russia's War in Ukraine," *New York Times*, September 26, 2023.

Lapowski, Issie, "NATO Group Catfished Soldiers to Prove a Point About Privacy," *Wired*, February 18, 2019.

Liedke, Jacob, and Galen Stocking, "Key Facts About Telegram," Pew Research Center, December 16, 2022.

Livieratos, Cole, "Cutting Army Special Operations Will Erode the Military's Ability to Influence the Modern Battlefield," *War on the Rocks*, January 9, 2024.

Loucaides, Darren, "How Telegram Became a Terrifying Weapon in the Israel-Hamas War," *Wired*, February 8, 2022.

Maddox, JD, Casi Gentzel, and Adela Levis, "Toward a Whole-of-Society Framework for Countering Disinformation," Modern War Institute, May 10, 2021.

Malaret, Jacqueline, and Ingrid Dickinson, "Yandex Suppresses Ukraine War Information for Russian Internet Users," Medium, March 31, 2022.

Marine Corps Doctrine Publication 8, *Information*, Department of the Navy, June 2022.

Martin, Diego A., Jacob N. Shapiro, and Julia G. Ihardt, "Introducing the Online Political Influence Efforts Dataset," *Journal of Peace Research*, Vol. 60, No. 5, November 2022.

Meta, "Bringing Local Context to Our Global Standards," webpage, January 18, 2023. As of February 15, 2024:
https://transparency.fb.com/policies/improving/bringing-local-context

Meta, "How Meta's Third-Party Fact-Checking Program Works," webpage, June 1, 2021. As of February 15, 2024:
https://www.facebook.com/formedia/blog/third-party-fact-checking-how-it-works

Metz, Sam, and Bouazza Ben Bouazza, "Russia's Foreign Minister Tours North Africa as Anger Toward the West Swells Across the Region," AP News, December 21, 2023.

Miller, Christopher, "'I Want to Live': Russians Defect to Ukraine by Calling Army Hotline," *Financial Times*, January 4, 2024.

Miller, Greg, "Panel Casts Doubt Against U.S. Propaganda Efforts Against ISIS," *Washington Post*, December 2, 2015.

Milmo, Dan, "Russia Blocks Access to Twitter and Facebook," *The Guardian*, March 4, 2022.

Myers, Steven Lee, "Russia Reactivates Its Trolls and Bots Ahead of Tuesday's Midterms," *New York Times*, November 10, 2022.

Myers, Steven Lee, "State Dept.'s Fight Against Disinformation Comes Under Attack," *New York Times*, December 14, 2023.

Nabozhniak, Oleksii, Oleksandra Tsekhanovska, Andrea Castagna, Dmytro Khutkyy, and Anna Melenchuk, *Revealing Russian Influence in Europe: Insights from Germany, France, Italy and Ukraine*, German Marshall Fund of the United States, 2023. As of April 9, 2024:
https://www.gmfus.org/sites/default/files/2024-01/revealing-russian-propaganda-3%5B71%5D.pdf

(U) National Intelligence Council, *Foreign Threats to the 2022 US Elections*, December 23, 2022, Declassified on December 11, 2023. As of February 15, 2024:
https://www.odni.gov/files/ODNI/documents/assessments/NIC-Declassified-ICA-Foreign-Threats-to-the-2022-US-Elections-Dec2023.pdf

NATO Strategic Communications Centre of Excellence, *Analysis of Russia's Information Campaign Against Ukraine*, 2015. As of March 22, 2024: https://stratcomcoe.org/cuploads/pfiles/russian_information_campaign _public_12012016fin.pdf

"New Slovak Government Rejects Final Military Aid Package for Ukraine," Reuters, November 8, 2023.

Nilar, Amani, "Ukraine Defence Ministry Sets Up Hotline for Family Members of Russian Soldiers," News 1st, February 27, 2022. As of February 14, 2024: https://www.newsfirst.lk/2022/02/27/ukraine-defence-ministry-sets-up-hotline -for-family-members-of-russian-soldiers

NORC, "New Survey Finds Most Russians See Ukrainian War as Defense Against West," press release, January 9, 2024.

Norton, Tim, "Fact Check: Did Zelensky's Wife Spend $1.1 Million at Cartier in New York?" *Newsweek*, October 5, 2023.

Nussbaum, Ania, and Samy Adghirni, "Macron Makes Ukraine Central in the European Election Campaign," Bloomberg, March 12, 2024.

Osadchuk, Roman, *Undermining Ukraine: How the Kremlin Employs Information Operations to Erode Global Confidence in Ukraine*, Atlantic Council, 2023. As of February 14, 2024: https://www.atlanticcouncil.org/wp-content/uploads/2023/02/Undermining -Ukraine-Final.pdf

Pamment, James, "RESIST 2 Counter Disinformation Toolkit," webpage, UK Government Communication Service, 2021. As of February 15, 2024: https://gcs.civilservice.gov.uk/publications/resist-2-counter-disinformation -toolkit/

Paul, Christopher, and Miriam Matthews, *The Russian "Firehose of Falsehood" Propaganda Model: Why It Might Work and Options to Counter It*, RAND, PE-198-OSD, 2016. As of June 7, 2024: https://www.rand.org/pubs/perspectives/PE198.html

Peltier, Elian, "Russia's Foreign Minister Heads to Mali, His Third Trip to Africa in Recent Months," *New York Times*, February 6, 2023.

Peltier, Elian, Adam Satariano, and Lynsey Chutel, "How Putin Became a Hero on African TV," *New York Times*, April 13, 2023.

Perfiliev, Sergei [@perfiliev], "A Ukrainian farmer using his tractor stole A TANK . . . 😂😂😂," Twitter post, February 27, 2022. As of February 15, 2024: https://twitter.com/perfiliev/status/1498024317594001409

Pifer, Steven, "Watch Out for Little Green Men," Brookings, July 7, 2014.

Pignal, Stanley, "Europe's Elections Pitch Centrists Against Populists, Again," *The Economist*, November 13, 2023.

Pitofsky, Marina, "A Girl Sang 'Let It Go' from 'Frozen' in a Bomb Shelter. Idina Menzel Says 'We See You,'" *USA Today*, March 9, 2022.

"Putin Approves New Media Restrictions Ahead of Presidential Election," *Al Jazeera*, November 14, 2023.

Rid, Thomas, *Active Measures: The Secret History of Disinformation and Political Warfare*, New York: Farrar, Straus and Giroux, 2020.

Robinson, Linda, Todd C. Helmus, Raphael S. Cohen, Alireza Nader, Andrew Radin, Madeline Magnuson, and Katya Migacheva, *Modern Political Warfare: Current Practices and Possible Responses*, RAND, RR-1772-A, 2018. As of February 15, 2024:
https://www.rand.org/pubs/research_reports/RR1772.html

Roozenbeek, Jon, Sander van der Linden, Beth Goldberg, Steve Rathje, and Stephan Lewandowsky, "Psychological Inoculation Improves Resilience Against Misinformation on Social Media," *Science Advances*, Vol. 8, No. 34, August 24, 2022.

Roth, Andrew, "In New Sanctions List, Ukraine Targets Russian Social-Media Sites," *Washington Post*, May 16, 2017.

Rothschild, Neal, "World Looks Elsewhere as Ukraine War Hits 100 Days," Axios, June 2, 2022.

Roussi, Antoaneta, and Jacopo Barigazzi, "Expect Russia to Do 'Whatever Possible' to Reassert Influence in Bulgaria, Outgoing PM Warns," *Politico*, April 9, 2024.

Ruban, Oleksandr, "Domestic Foreign Broadcasting of Ukraine. Whom Do the State TV Channels 'Dim' and 'FreeDom' Broadcast To?" ["Внутрішнє іномовлення України. На кого мовлять державні телеканали 'Дім' і 'FreeДом'"], webpage, Institute of Mass Information, December 4, 2023. As of June 7, 2024:
https://imi.org.ua/monitorings/vnutrishnye-inomovlennya-ukrayiny-na-kogo
-movlyat-derzhavni-telekanaly-dim-i-freedom-i57418

Rudik, Kira [@kira.rudik], "Ukrainian woman. I love colorful tulips, pilates, the color pink. Planting flowers, walking until night on Andriivskyi, my cat Michelle. Smelling new perfumes, laughing out loud, wearing soft socks that are a little slippery on the floor. Wiping glasses with a napkin, marshmallows, arranging documents alphabetically" ["українська жінка. Я люблю різнокольорові тюльпани, пілатес, рожевий колір. Саджати квіти, гуляти до ночі по андріївському, свою кішку Мішель. Нюхати нові парфуми, голосно сміятись, носити м'які шкарпетки, які трохи слизькі на підлозі. Витирати серветкою бокали, зефір, розкладати документи за алфавітом"], Instagram post, February 25, 2022. As of June 7, 2024:
https://www.instagram.com/p/CaaC01QKxOI/?utm_source=ig_embed&ig
_rid=6df50605-9940-4d45-8529-7ac7f667d6e4

"Russian Media Regulator Blocks More Online News Sources over Coverage of Ukraine War," Radio Free Europe/Radio Liberty, March 16, 2022.

Ryan, Missy, Ellen Nakashima, Michael Birnbaum, and David L. Stern, "Outmatched in Military Might, Ukraine Has Excelled in the Information War," *Washington Post*, March 16, 2022.

Sato, Mia, "Ukrainian Influencers Bring the Frontlines to TikTok," *The Verge*, March 16, 2022.

Serhan, Yasmeen, "As Russian's War Enters Third Year, Optimism for Ukraine Sinks," *Time*, February 23, 2024.

Shevchenko, Anastasiia, "Mapping of Telegram Channels in Ukraine, a Year into the Full-Scale War," *The Fix*, April 21, 2023.

Silverman, Adam, "Thinking Security: Black Psyops, Laundering Misinformation, Disinformation, & Agitprop," Ark Valley Voice, November 30, 2019.

Silverman, Jacob, "That Propaganda Program Bill Clinton Praised Hillary For? It Was Considered a Failure," *Politico*, July 27, 2016.

Singer, Peter W., and Eric B. Johnson, "The Need to Inoculate Military Servicemembers Against Information Threats: The Case for Digital Literacy Training for the Force," *War on the Rocks*, February 1, 2021.

Sologoub, Ilona, "Attitudes of Ukrainians Towards Russia and Russians Towards Ukraine" ["Stavlennia ukraintsiv do Rosii ta rosiian do Ukrainy"], VoxUkraine, June 24, 2023.

Spravdi, "About the Centre," webpage, undated. As of February 15, 2024: https://spravdi.gov.ua/en/about-us/

Srivastava, Mehul, "'Trolling Helps Show the King Has No Clothes': How Ukraine's Army Conquered Twitter," *Financial Times*, October 14, 2022.

Stoklasa, Radovan, and Jan Lopatka, "Pellegrini Wins Slovak Presidential Election in Boost for Pro-Russian PM Fico," Reuters, April 6, 2024.

Stone, Peter, "Russia Disinformation Looks to US Far Right to Weaken Ukraine Support," *The Guardian*, March 16, 2023.

StopFake, "Tools," webpage, undated. As of February 15, 2024: https://www.stopfake.org/en/category/tools/

Sukhankin, Sergey, "Russia Struggles for 'Hearts and Minds' in Global South (Part Two)," Jamestown Foundation, February 23, 2024.

Sullivan, Kate, and Shania Shelton, "Trump Signals Opposition to New Senate Foreign Aid Package," CNN, February 10, 2024.

Susman-Peña, Tara, and Katya Vogt, "Ukrainians' Self-Defense Against Disinformation: What We Learned from Learn to Discern," webpage, International Research and Exchanges Board, June 12, 2017. As of February 15, 2024:
https://www.irex.org/insight/ukrainians-self-defense-against-disinformation -what-we-learned-learn-discern

Synyts'ka, Daryna, "Over UAH 900 Million Were Paid for Telethons and Programs for 'Dom,' FreeDom and the Gaze" ["Понад 900 млн грн за рік заплатили за телемарафони й програми для 'Дому,' FreeДом та The Gaze"], *Dozorro*, February 22, 2024. As of March 22, 2024:
https://dozorro.org/blog/ponad-900-mln-grn-za-rik-zaplatili-za-telemarafoni -j-programi-dlya-domu-freedom-ta-gaze

Trebesch, Christoph, Arianna Antezza, Katelyn Bushnell, André Frank, Pascal Frank, Lukas Franz, Ivan Kharitonov, Bharath Kumar, Ekaterina Rebinskaya, and Stefan Schramm, "The Ukraine Support Tracker: Which Countries Help Ukraine and How?" Kiel Institute for the World Economy, Kiel Working Paper No. 2218, February 23, 2023. As of February 15, 2024:
https://www.ifw-kiel.de/fileadmin/Dateiverwaltung/IfW-Publications/fis -import/87bb7b0f-ed26-4240-8979-5e6601aea9e8-KWP_2218_Trebesch_et _al_Ukraine_Support_Tracker.pdf

Trevelyan, Mark, and Kevin Liffey, "African Leaders Tell Putin: 'We Have a Right to Call for Peace,'" Reuters, July 28, 2023.

Treyger, Elina, Joe Cheravitch, and Raphael S. Cohen, *Russian Disinformation Efforts on Social Media*, RAND, RR-4373/2-AF, 2022. As of June 7, 2024:
https://www.rand.org/pubs/research_reports/RR4373z2.html

Troianovski, Anton, and Valeriya Safronova, "Russia Takes Censorship to New Extremes, Stifling War Coverage," *New York Times*, March 4, 2022.

Tropynina, Alina, "The Ability of Ukrainians to Distinguish Messages of Russian Propaganda: Results of Public Opinion Research," VoxUkraine, June 26, 2023.

Tsybulska, Liubov [@TsybulskaLiubov], "In Kyiv a woman knocked down a Russian drone from a balcony with a jar of cucumbers. How did they expect to occupy this country?" post to the X platform, March 5, 2022. As of February 15, 2024:
https://twitter.com/TsybulskaLiubov/status/1500075457798189057

Ukraine Crisis Media Center, "Who We Are," webpage, undated. As of February 15, 2023:
https://uacrisis.org/en/pro-nas

U.S. Embassy and Consulates in Italy, "How Russia Conducts False Flag Operations," webpage, undated. As of February 15, 2024:
https://it.usembassy.gov/how-russia-conducts-false-flag-operations/

U.S. Government Accountability Office, *Information Environment Opportunities and Threats to DOD's National Security Mission*, GAO-22-104714, September 2022. As of April 16, 2024:
https://www.gao.gov/assets/gao-22-104714.pdf

Vigers, Benedict, "Ukrainians Stand Behind War Effort Despite Some Fatigue," Gallup, October 9, 2023.

Vock, Ido, "Russian Network That 'Paid European Politicians' Busted, Authorities Claim," BBC News, March 28, 2024.

Walter, N., J. J. Brooks, C. J. Saucier, and S. Suresh, "Evaluating the Impact of Attempts to Correct Health Misinformation on Social Media: A Meta-Analysis," *Health Communication*, Vol. 36, No. 13, November 2021.

Walton, Calder, "False-Flag Invasions Are a Russian Specialty," *Foreign Policy*, February 4, 2022.

We Are Ukraine, homepage, undated. As of June 10, 2024:
https://www.weareukraine.info

We Dream and Act [Мріємо і діємо], "Summing up the Results of the National Media Literacy Test 2023 . . ." ["Підбиваємо Підсумки Національного Тесту з Медіаграмотності 2023 . . ."], Facebook post, November 2, 2023. As of June 7, 2024:
https://www.facebook.com/watch/?v=306746648818327

Wilson Center, "Media Bans, Free Speech, and Disinformation in Ukraine," webcast event, March 12, 2021. As of February 15, 2024:
https://www.wilsoncenter.org/event/media-bans-free-speech-and-disinformation
-ukraine

Yohannes-Kassahun, Bitsat, "One Year Later: The Impact of the Russian Conflict with Ukraine on Africa," *Africa Renewal*, February 13, 2023. As of April 16, 2024:
https://www.un.org/africarenewal/magazine/february-2023/one-year-later
-impact-russian-conflict-ukraine-africa

York, Joanna, "'World's First TikTok War': Ukraine's Social Media Campaign 'a Question of Survival,'" France 24, February 2, 2023.

Younis, Mohamed, "Confidence in U.S. Military Lowest in over Two Decades," Gallup, July 31, 2023.